Death of a Traveller

Death of a Traveller

A Counter-Investigation

Didier Fassin

Translated by Rachel Gomme

polity

First published in French as *Mort d'un voyageur: une contre-enquête*
© Seuil 2020

First published in English in 2021 by Polity Press

Polity Press
65 Bridge Street
Cambridge CB2 1UR, UK

Polity Press
101 Station Landing
Suite 300
Medford, MA 02155, USA

ISBN-13: 978-1-5095-4740-1
ISBN-13: 978-1-5095-4741-8 (pb)

A catalogue record for this book is available from the British Library.

Library of Congress Cataloging-in-Publication Data

Names: Fassin, Didier, author.
Title: Death of a traveller : a counter investigation / Didier Fassin ;
   translated by Rachel Gomme.
Other titles: Mort d'un voyageur. English
Description: Medford : Polity Press, 2021. | Includes bibliographical
   references. | Summary: "A leading anthropologist shows how the police
   and the justice system work against marginalized communities"-- Provided
   by publisher.
Identifiers: LCCN 2020046192 (print) | LCCN 2020046193 (ebook) | ISBN
   9781509547401 (hardback) | ISBN 9781509547418 (paperback) | ISBN
   9781509547425 (epub) | ISBN 9781509548071 (pdf)
Subjects: LCSH: Discrimination in criminal justice
   administration--France--Case studies. | Romanies--Crimes against. |
   Homicide--France--Case studies. | Police shootings--France--Case
   studies. | Romanies--France--Social conditions. | Minorities--Crimes
   against--France | Minorities--Legal status, laws, etc.--France.
Classification: LCC HV9960.F8 F3713 2021 (print) | LCC HV9960.F8 (ebook)
   | DDC 364.152092--dc23
LC record available at https://lccn.loc.gov/2020046192
LC ebook record available at https://lccn.loc.gov/2020046193

Typeset in 11 on 13 pt Sabon by
Servis Filmsetting Ltd, Stockport, Cheshire
Printed and bound in Great Britain by TJ Books Limited

For further information on Polity, visit our website: politybooks.com

For Angelo's sister, for his parents,
and for all those who fight for truth and justice
on behalf of the ones injured or killed by the police

The truth was a mirror in the hands of God. It fell, and broke into pieces. Everybody took a piece of it, and they looked at it and thought they had the truth.

Djalâl al-Dîn Muhammad Rûmî

The *more* affects we are able to put into words about a thing, the *more* eyes, various eyes we are able to use for the same thing, the more complete will be our 'concept' of the thing, our 'objectivity'.

Friedrich Nietzsche

Contents

Acknowledgments ix
A Simple Story: Preface to the English Edition xi
Terminological Note xx
Preamble xxiii

Prologue. 1

    I The Father 11

   II The First Officer 16

  III The Mother. 21

  IV The Second Officer 26

    V The Doctor 30

  VI The Sister 34

 VII The Prosecutor 39

VIII The Journalist. 47

  IX Dignity 51

    X Campaign 58

  XI Mourning 65

XII Biography 70

XIII Investigation 77

XIV Dismissal........................... 82

XV Truth 90

XVI Lies................................ 96

XVII Reconstruction 104

XVIII That Day........................... 116

Epilogue................................. 125

Acknowledgments

This project would not have been undertaken without the collaboration of Angelo's family. I am profoundly grateful for the trust they placed in me throughout my work and for the integrity they showed, in spite of the pain this story still aroused in them more than two years after the tragedy. My thanks are also due to the other people involved in this case, particularly in the Justice and Truth Collective. I am equally indebted to the lawyers and magistrates who gave me the benefit of their insight and their skill as well as their view of the victim, the events that led to his death and the judicial procedure that followed, and in particular to the public prosecutor who generously granted me access to the case file. Having chosen to maintain the anonymity of the protagonists and not to name the places where they live and work, I cannot express my gratitude to them by name.

The research on which this book is based was supported by funds from the NOMIS Foundation within the context of a research program I designed around the theme of crisis. The warm welcome this unconventional project received from Séverine Nikel at Le Seuil, before even a single line had been written, played an important role in my decision to carry it through, and our subsequent discussions helped me to clarify my position in this experimental writing. It is a pleasure for me to have it now published by Polity, and I am thankful to John Thompson for having fast-tracked its publication. The translation made by Rachel Gomme is once more remarkable for its attentiveness to the slightest semantic inflections in the text. And Munirah Bishop's help has been, as always, precious.

Finally, the almost daily conversations I had with Anne-Claire Defossez throughout the period of writing, and her comments on the book, helped me to resolve a number of problems that I faced, to reorient myself when I went off track, to clear the doubts that obscured the way forward, and – without reaching them – to test the limits of her patience.

A Simple Story

Preface to the English Edition

It is a simple story. Somewhere in France, a man from the Traveller community is sought after he fails to return from home leave to the prison where he has been serving time for a number of robberies that did not involve violence. As he is visiting with his parents at the family farm, an elite unit of the gendarmerie, the GIGN, heavily equipped and armed, launches a major operation. Hiding in the dark in a lean-to, he is discovered and killed. The men who shot him assert that he attacked them with a knife and they were obliged to fire in legitimate self-defense, but not before they had announced their presence and attempted to bring him under control without the use of weapons. Five members of his family who are present outside the lean-to, held handcuffed on the ground at machinegun point a few yards from the site of the events, maintain that the shots came only a few seconds after the gendarmes entered the lumber room, without either warning or the sounds of a struggle. An inquiry is immediately opened by the national gendarmerie's investigation department; its conclusions support the account given by their colleagues. The public prosecutor makes a statement that reiterates this version but, because a man has died, requests a judicial investigation. Taking into consideration some troubling elements in witness statements and expert witness reports, the examining magistrate decides to place the two officers who fired the shots under investigation. However, eighteen months later, just before giving her ruling, she is transferred to another jurisdiction. The colleague who takes over from her is in her first posting as examining magistrate and has to draw up the final ruling immediately after her appointment. She follows the public prosecutor's analysis and dismisses the case. The family lodges an appeal. It ends with the same ruling. The two GIGN men who fired the fatal shots will therefore never be brought to trial. Deeply traumatized by her brother's death, suspecting from the outset that the gendarmes are lying, and shocked by the speed with which the public prosecutor moved to validate their version of the events, Angelo's sister commits publicly to ensuring that, as she puts it, the truth is told and justice done. She takes the lead in a local campaign that echoes those led by other young women whose brothers have also died in interactions with law enforcement without the officers involved in these deaths ever being convicted. When the final appeal is rejected by the Court of Cassation she submits a petition to the European Court of Human Rights, in the hope that it will issue a judgment against the French state both for the circumstances of her brother's death and for the way the justice system proceeded in exonerating the gendarmes who killed him.

A simple story, then. A minor incident that did not even merit a mention in the national media. Only the local newspaper reported it, in brief articles that reiterated the public prosecutor's version without any attempt to inquire into the family's testimony. Yet what merits attention is precisely the fact that it is such a routine occurrence. Its apparent insignificance is what makes it significant. It combines all the elements present in any number of similar incidents that take place every day throughout the world: young men belonging to ethnic minorities who die as a result of encounters with the police; inquiries conducted by colleagues of the presumed perpetrators who confirm their account of the events; prosecutors and judges who decide not to pursue the case and accept their claim of legitimate self-defense. No homicide, therefore no case to answer. Lives stolen without justice being done. But, beyond this common set of circumstances, what makes this incident exemplary is, on the one hand, the normalization of deployment of special units and their disproportionate use of force as standard procedure in poor neighborhoods with a high ethnic minority population and, on the other, the increasingly generalized use of incarceration in response to offenses committed by lower-income sectors of society, contrasting with the leniency the law and judges exhibit toward crime and criminality among the privileged classes.

Such tragedies have long remained invisible to the majority of the population. The official versions justified punitive practices by stigmatizing the victims and exonerating the police officers responsible in the name of public order. But in recent years political campaigns have brought them into the foreground. In the United States, there is the Black Lives Matter movement, which burgeoned after Michael Brown was killed by a police officer in Ferguson, Missouri, in 2014. In France, the Justice and Truth committees have become vocal, the best known of which concerns Adama Traoré, who died in the police station at Beaumont-sur-Oise shortly after his arrest in 2016. Above all, the images of the dying moments of George Floyd, suffocated by a police officer in Minneapolis on 25 May 2020, have given this tragic event a worldwide impact, resonating with the police violence toward minorities experienced in many countries. What was until recently a blind spot in the public space is now common knowledge. What societies had implicitly tolerated seems to have become intolerable. Angelo's death finds its place in this new moral economy, where what is at issue is not only the extinction of a life but also the indignity of the circumstances of this death, particularly the treatment of the deceased's body, and the institutional lies that usually allow those responsible to go unpunished, further sullying the victim's memory. Like a modern Antigone, the sister fights to restore respectability to her dead brother and, through him, to the Travellers, who are continually stigmatized and discriminated against, and she thus stands against all the Creons who lay claim to public authority.

But how can an account of this tragedy be rendered without eliding the issues involved? Is there a way to escape having to choose between outraged condemnation of an injustice and a bare description of the facts? This is a classic dilemma for social scientists, who often profess the value neutrality advocated by Max Weber, yet are aware that they are bound up in what Norbert Elias described as an involved epistemology. Over recent decades the answer has continually oscillated: in the French context, the tension is between the critical sociology of Pierre Bourdieu, declared to expose hidden power relations, and the pragmatic sociology of Luc Boltanski, supposed to establish a pure grammar of action and justifications for it, which dominated their field alternately in the late twentieth century. Rather than asserting that a solution to this dilemma has been found, it can be fruitful to take the view that this is an aporia which needs to be treated as such.

On this basis, I therefore proposed to approach Angelo's death from two distinct directions. In the first stage, I strove to reproduce each of the testimonies gathered by the investigators and by myself, not only from those present at the scene but also from people who became involved later, so as to give an account from each individual's point of view, whether that of the sister, the medical doctor, the public prosecutor, the local journalist or the examining magistrates. In the second stage, I attempted to carry out anew the investigation, drawing on all the available material, from records of depositions to expert witness reports, so as to produce a reconstruction of the events that, being based purely on empirical data, is as free as possible of bias and pressure. The writing strategy I have devised is therefore experimental. It seeks first to avoid the false objectivity of any unequivocal statement of the facts, as I give space to discordant voices and incompatible versions. It then makes it possible to do away with a comfortable relativism that would be limited to parsing each individual's argument, since at the end of my analysis I propose an account of the events as they might plausibly have unfolded. My aim therefore is to open up the black box of the functioning of the state, more specifically its law-enforcement mechanisms, the police and the justice system, rather than adopting the position habitually taken by the social sciences on the outside. To put it another way, my aim is to investigate the investigation, and to do so by revealing what the judges caused to disappear. This is a delicate process and a risky endeavor, though. The judicial investigation is indeed legally protected by judicial confidentiality that may be lifted only by the public prosecutor. By dismissing the case, and consequently preventing a trial from being held, the examining magistrate removed the case from public view. By reopening the file, I make the various elements in it accessible to readers.

The field of research in which I present my proposition thus sits on the boundary between history and literature, between law and journalism. It is not a new one, but it is one that I invite readers to explore afresh. Michel Foucault recounts how, when he discovered the story of an early nineteenth-century parricide whose astonishing memoir describes how he committed a triple murder in his own family, he and the students in his seminar fell under the spell of both the case and the text. The story immediately aroused his interest, but it also moved him. It enthralled him, in the strong sense of the word, on both these levels. It was only later that he decided, with his young colleagues, to publish *I, Pierre Rivière, Having Slaughtered My Mother, My Sister and My Brother . . .,* gathering together the extant documents, including the famous memoir, and adding a series of notes that effectively represent the reflections of the researchers in this little group. The aim, one of them later noted, was to make all the material in the case file available to the public. I think I can say that my relationship to Angelo's story followed the same course. The circumstances of his death attracted my attention, while the courage and determination demonstrated by his sister aroused my sympathy. The idea of making it the subject of research and of a book came to me only a year later, here too in order to enable a broad audience to form their own view of what really happened in the lean-to that day, and what could possibly explain the great disproportionality between the crimes with which the young man was reproached and his eventual fate. Unlike the collective of authors at the Collège de France, I have not published the documents themselves, which would have been against the law, but I have integrated them into the accounts I have put together and the counter-investigation I have conducted.

The published archive therefore comprises not raw material but, rather, narratives and analyses drawn from it. As far as the narratives are concerned, the reconstitution of the various versions is akin to the literary form of the non-fiction novel, and the reference that immediately comes to mind is *In Cold Blood*, in which Truman Capote recounts a quadruple murder that took place in a small town in Kansas. Asserting that everything contained in this account derives from his own observations, his interviews and official records, he usually adopts the position of omniscient narrator, producing a third-person account that alternates the points of view of the murderers, the victims, the police and others related to the crime and criminals. Since the crime has been solved, the perpetrators having confessed, he is able to construct a coherent narrative. For my own part, while I draw on similar kinds of empirical material and alternate the viewpoints of eight individuals more or less directly involved in the events, I do not pass over the inconsistencies in these versions, which, at least as far as Angelo's death is concerned, are irreconcilable. Since the circumstances in which the gendarmes were led to open fire were never fully elucidated, I give readers the opportunity to follow the trail and grasp the experience of each of the protagonists as they describe it, without prejudging the veracity of their account. What I am writing is not a novel but an investigation. As far as the analysis is concerned, the exploration of the various modalities of truth, the deconstruction of the rationales for lying among the police, the flaws in the investigation and the justifications for the dismissal of the case resemble the means in a work of detection, similar to the method by which Carlo Ginzburg proceeds in *The Judge and the Historian*. His book was written in defense of his friend Adriano Sofri, who was accused of having organized, sixteen years earlier, the execution of a police chief himself suspected of being responsible for the death of an anarchist. To this end, Ginzburg points out the implausibilities and contradictions in the suspect avowals of the informer who accused three of his former Lotta Continua comrades in exchange for a suspension of sentence for his own involvement, and he discusses the question of evidence and proofs, which are necessarily treated in different ways depending on whether one is conducting a trial or undertaking research, as the title of the book suggests. Although the event under consideration and the judicial process are very different in my case, I proceed similarly to a counter-investigation. However, I do so not having decided in advance that the gendarmes did not fire in legitimate self-defense but by systematically taking up each piece of evidence the judges drew on or, conversely, ignored in their process of establishing what they call judicial truth. It is what ultimately leads me to propose another interpretation of the facts, one that pays more attention to the improbabilities and contradictions in the official version and that aligns better with the existing evidence and proofs.

What fascinated Foucault and his fellow researchers in the story of Pierre Rivière was the process of veridiction at work, among the doctors, judges and the murderer himself, in a case that combined crime and madness, criminal responsibility and mental health. What drove Capote's investigation and Ginzburg's counter-investigation was the possibility of drawing out a truth, in the first case through literature, in the second in the name of justice. These, then, are two distinct projects with regard to the question of truth-telling: for Foucault and his colleagues it is the interplay of utterances of truth that interests them; for Capote and Ginzburg it is the truth itself that is at stake. The present book moves progressively from the former to the latter, from the operation of veridiction toward the search for truth. This truth, which I have called ethnographic truth, is independent of the relations of power and knowledge underlying the production of judicial truth. It has no argument to make apart from the fact that it arises out of the twofold decision to give all accounts the same credit and to rely solely on assessment of the evidence. Deliberately limited in its ambition, this version, unlike the judicial truth, has no bearing on recognition of the guilt or innocence of those accused. But it has weight for those to whom truth is habitually denied, for it restores some part of their dignity and even offers them a glimpse of the hope of justice. While it has no impact in the courts, it partakes of an ethical concern.

This concern is a live one. It articulates a matter of urgency. While the death of men in interactions with the police is a frequent occurrence generally fostered by the exoneration of the alleged perpetrators, it is rare to have access to all the evidence in one of these cases, and even exceptional when the case has been dismissed because it is then subject to judicial confidentiality, breach of which is punishable in France by one year's imprisonment and a fine of €15,000. Having been granted authorization to consult the documents in the case concerning Angelo's death, I have therefore felt an obligation to put this privilege to good use by seeing this work through. Apart from the singularity of the case, starting with the fact that it concerns a Traveller, with all the marginality, suspicion and ostracism implied by that identity, it seemed to me that, both in the method of intervention chosen to effect the young man's arrest and in the logic of the judicial process that culminated in the absolution of the two men who fired the fatal shots, there were a number of features that could be identified or inferred in many other cases throughout the world. The details of these cases may vary, but they are tragically alike in their dénouement: the loss of a life and the impunity of those responsible. In this respect the simple story of the death of Angelo, extended through his sister's fight for justice and truth, acquires if not a universal then at least an exemplary significance.

D.F., August 2020

Terminological Note

The organization of law enforcement and the operation of the judicial system is specific to each country, and even sometimes to each jurisdiction within a given country, as in the United States. Some explanations are therefore in order so as to make the account that follows clear for readers unfamiliar with the French systems.

In France there are two main law-enforcement institutions, which have roughly equivalent authority but distinct legal status and territories of operation. The national police is a civilian force that operates within cities and on their outskirts. The national gendarmerie is a military force operating in rural areas and small towns. There are also municipal police forces under the authority of local mayors, whose role is more limited, complementing the two other forces. In this text the generic term "police" is used to refer to law-enforcement bodies. Angelo's family, who live on a farm, have only ever had dealings with the gendarmerie, and the two who killed the young man were *adjudants* (non-commissioned officers), the first rank above beat officer. For the purposes of clarity, the translation uses the term *officers* for these two in order to distinguish them from the other gendarmes involved in the operation. All belong to an elite unit, the GIGN, or Groupe d'intervention de la gendarmerie nationale (National Gendarmerie Intervention Group), which was created to intervene in terrorist attacks, hostage situations and the fight against organized crime – in other words, circumstances very different from a simple arrest.

The judicial system in France, as in the majority of countries in continental Europe and their former colonies, is based on civil law, derived from Roman law, and thus quite different from the common law that operates in the United States, the United Kingdom and the Commonwealth. One notable feature is the stage of judicial investigation, prior to the trial at criminal court, that is instigated by the *procureur de la République* (public prosecutor), or requested by the victim(s), and is conducted by a *juge d'instruction* (examining magistrate). The latter's role is to establish whether a breach of the law has been committed and whether there is evidence to support charging the perpetrator(s). At the end of her or his investigation, after having received a statement (*réquisition*) from the public prosecutor and the responses (*observations*) from the counsels, the magistrate draws up a ruling (*ordonnance*), which may be either a dismissal (*non-lieu*), in which case there is no trial, or a referral to the criminal court (*renvoi*) where the accused will be tried. A decision to dismiss may be appealed in the same way as a court decision. If the decision or verdict is upheld on appeal, there remains the possibility of a petition to the Court of Cassation, but this court rules only on points of procedure, not on matters of substance; if procedural problems are confirmed, this leads to a new trial. One final stage, when all internal means of recourse are exhausted, is to appeal to the European Court of Human Rights, if the appellant considers that her or his rights have been violated. If the European Court rules in favor of the plaintiff, it may issue a decision against the state in question, accompanied by a requirement to pay the appellant a sum corresponding to the legal costs and to the material and moral harm suffered. However, such a decision does not mean that the case has to be retried and therefore does not expose the individuals charged to any form of judgment or sanction.

The victims in the present case belong to the social group known as *gens du voyage* (travelling people). Determining the right way to name them is always a sensitive matter, for there are several words whose definitions and implications vary depending on context and speaker. The choice has been made here to respect the way the protagonists identify themselves. As far as Angelo and his family are concerned, most of them think of themselves simply as *voyageurs* (Travellers). The term may seem paradoxical given that they are settled, but it is noteworthy that, at the family property, a former farm, all prefer to sleep in caravans rather than in the buildings, testimony to a sort of nostalgia for a traveling way of life despite the fact that some of them have never known it. They sometimes use the term *manouche* when speaking about themselves, but never *rom* (Roma) or *gitan* (gypsy), since the former relates in their eyes to a specific community and the latter has pejorative connotations. While the translation of the book uses US English, the British English writing of the term "Traveller" has been preferred to differentiate it from the word "traveler," which refers to a person who is traveling. The double "l" signifies the identity of a group.

Preamble

This is a book of a singular kind. It is not the result of a traditional sociological investigation. It is a counter-investigation. I explain how it arose in the prologue. It seeks to shed light on the death of a man through the accounts of those who killed him and those who were more or less immediate witnesses to the scene. It also attempts to analyze the judicial handling of the case up until it was dismissed, those who fired the fatal shots being exculpated on grounds of legitimate self-defense. Inset between these two elements is a description of the reactions of the deceased man's family and a reconstruction of the victim's life story. I present the accounts of the protagonists as faithfully as possible through the use of a subjective, third-person narrative. By contrast, I examine the judicial process through a critical lens, in order to show how choices were made early on between irreconcilable versions of the story, resulting in problematic decisions. On the basis of a re-examination of the individual accounts and the case file, I then propose a different version of the facts that makes it possible to integrate the contradictions, divergences and discrepancies that remain in the judges' interpretation. The aim is thus to create, around this tragic case, an experimental form of writing that honors the diverse viewpoints, as evoked

in the epigraph from Rumi, while at the same time ultimately acknowledging my own perspective, at the end of
an inquiry inspired by the quotation from Nietzsche. The
unusual approach I have adopted raises two questions.

First, can I be said to take sides? This is a charge readily leveled against sociologists and anthropologists, who
are often suspected of taking the part of the dominated.
The observation is not entirely without foundation, and
there is, moreover, no such thing as total impartiality.
But here the opposite argument is called for. Once the
magistrates have fully accepted one version of the events
and rejected the other, the simple fact of giving equal
weight to each, as I do here, and thus presenting them
as both equally credible, tends to be seen as a failure of
impartiality, whereas in fact it testifies to an effort to
restore it. In this respect I show, in the sections focusing
on the conditions of production of truth and lies in legal
cases, that this case is far from an anomaly. It is not the
exception, but the rule. It reveals not a dysfunctional
justice system but its normal functioning, which needs
to be analyzed as such if we are to understand the logics
that prevail in the handling of such cases.

Second, is this work still one of social science?
Admittedly, it does not follow the traditional forms of
the discipline. Subjective recounting of the facts belongs
to literature, the conduct of the inquiry is reminiscent of
a particular kind of journalism, and the reconstruction of
the investigation without doubt echoes the form of the
criminal investigation process. These comparisons are
reasonable, in my view, and in no way discreditable. But
I contend that I maintain certain fundamental principles
of the social sciences: empirical research based on a field
study supplemented by examination of documents; equal
attention accorded to the words of all those involved; a
commitment to subject all available evidence to critical
examination; the desire to go beyond the individual case
and reveal the generality of social processes; and, indeed,
the acknowledgment of the presence of the researcher,

whom I have chosen to present from the outset as one protagonist among others.

Although the criminal investigation is long since over, the dismissal of the case was confirmed on appeal, and the petition to the Court of Cassation was judged inadmissible, it is probable that the case will be referred to the European Court of Human Rights. The way I have written it, presenting an honest reconstruction of the points of view of the main protagonists and a rigorous analysis of all the evidence in the investigation case file, and eventually putting forward an account of the events that differs from that of the justice system, takes this possibility into account.

Prologue

It appeared to me that the examining magistrate had not deciphered the problem at the root of this case, and I thought it might be of interest if I contributed here the information resulting from my own deciphering of it.

Fernando Pessoa, *Il Caso Vargas*

One morning, the sociologist receives an email from a collective that has come together to seek justice following the death of a Traveller. He has never heard of the case. He does not know the three persons who sign the email, all women. They give a succinct account of the tragic death of a thirty-seven-year-old man, the brother of one of them. He was killed by officers from the GIGN, Groupe d'intervention de la gendarmerie nationale, a special unit of the gendarmerie dedicated to terrorist attacks and hostage situations, who had come to arrest him as he was deemed to have absconded because he had not returned to prison following home leave. The three women tell the sociologist that they have read some of his books, and they would like to invite him to participate in a panel discussion focused on ending state violence, as their press release puts it. Moved by the man's story, sympathetic to the collective's campaign, and baffled by the implausibility

of the official version of the events – all factors that echo
other cases in which he has taken an interest – the sociologist nevertheless replies that, unfortunately, as he is not
in France, he must decline their invitation. A few moments
later, however, he follows up with a postscript proposing
to write a short text that they could read at the event if they
wish. They accept with enthusiasm. He therefore sends
them a few pages in which he reflects on the machinery of
law enforcement, penal structures and the prison system
in France, where recent developments have led to tragedies
such as the one in which this man died. Indeed, this tragic
event sits at the intersection of ethnographic research he
has been conducting for some fifteen years on the police,
courts and prisons. The deceased man's sister writes a
brief message to say that she was touched when she read
the text, as since her brother's death she has been feeling a powerful need to articulate these things but knows
that, when spoken by Travellers, they go unheard. She
adds that she shared the text with her father, who himself
experienced prison from the age of thirteen: after listening
attentively he told her that he approved of what it said.
The short address is therefore included in the program for
the event. A slightly amended version is published a few
weeks later on the first anniversary of the tragedy, as an
opinion column in a national daily newspaper.

Over the following months, the sociologist continues
to receive the collective's regular press releases. He is
thus kept informed about the judicial process, the hopes
raised when those who fired the shots are placed under
investigation and then dashed when the case is dismissed.
He learns also of the marches in memory of the victim
and in support of his family, held in the nearby administrative town where the case is to be decided as well as
in other places where similar tragedies have taken place.
After several email exchanges, he eventually goes to meet
with the Traveller's sister and other members of his family,
including his parents, in their village. Spending the day
with them, he takes note of the wound that remains open,

the anger at a justice system that did not listen to them, the grieving that cannot begin until their words have been heard. Thus is germinated the idea for a book that would respect their version of the tragedy they have lived, and are still living through. The proposal is still unformed, and the support not guaranteed, as he explains to them. But they accept the idea without hesitation. He tells them too that he cannot simply reproduce their view, that he will have to include accounts from other perspectives. And he speaks to them of his scruples about questioning them on such painful events, causing them to relive this traumatic recent past. It hurts to talk about it, they say, but it does us good all the same. In any case, we talk about it with each other every day. Every day we talk about it. A few weeks later, the sociologist writes to the family to tell them that his publisher is willing to publish the book. It is such a poignant day for us to receive that news, replies the Traveller's sister. Today would have been his fortieth birthday.

Thus begins an investigation, or rather a counter-investigation, that leads the sociologist to interrupt all his other projects for several months. The man's death and the ensuing criminal inquiry take a forceful hold on him – a sort of ethical urgency that cannot be put off. For, ultimately, this story is a tragic illustration of what has formed the substance of his two most recent books: the will to punish and the inequality of lives. He must once again return to examine the circumstances of this tragic event and the legal proceedings in order to understand what has played out here at both the specific and the generic level. He therefore conducts twelve interviews with the protagonists in the case, explaining his project clearly to each person so as to avoid any misunderstanding. The deceased's relatives and those involved either closely or more distantly in the events and its aftermath agree readily, as do the judges and lawyers, save one. Conversely, repeated approaches to the gendarmes, both individually and via their institution, both locally and at the national level, yield no result. Likewise multiple requests to some of the indirect witnesses, such as the emergency doctor, and to others having taken part in the story, such as the journalist. Thanks in particular to the diligence of the family and of the public prosecutor's office, documents are assembled: the five handwritten accounts by the parents, uncle, brother and sister-in-law, made just after the tragedy; the twenty-seven statements of witness depositions; the autopsy and ballistics reports, that of weapon examination, the toxicology and forensic analyses; the record of the reconstruction of the events and of the visit to the scene; the public prosecution's charges and the defense lawyers' responses; the ruling that dismissed the case and its upholding on appeal; the fourteen press releases from the support committee and the twenty-eight articles in the regional press. The pieces of the jigsaw gradually come together. Yet gaps remain, owing to questions that were not asked by the investigators, contradictions that were not brought up during the criminal investigation, points of vagueness and approximations in the various versions of the facts, silences and refusals to be interviewed. Thus, a rich but incomplete fabric is woven, in which the record of a deposition can partially fill in for the missing interview with the witnesses concerned.

But the point of this project is not to substitute the authority of the words written by the sociologist for the authority of the words spoken by the judge. The aim is first to do justice to all the versions of the events and then, on the basis of evidence collected, to formulate a plausible interpretation unfettered by the judicial decision. The relationships between the work of judge and that of historian have long been scrutinized, with the aim either of demonstrating the similarities between them or, on the contrary, to warn against a historiography that sets itself up as public prosecutor or defender of characters or events. Some historians have even gone so far as to re-examine court decisions in cases from their own times. In the present instance, there is something of a potential dialogue between the judge and the ethnographer, in which the ethnographer takes the liberty of investigating the judge's interpretation. A new form therefore needs to be essayed in order to produce accounts that keep as closely as possible to the facts as they emerge over the course of interviews, depositions, field observations and the assembly of other documentary traces, all the while embedding them in descriptions and narratives through a process of re-creation. Composing the text becomes an operation akin to jointing a brickwork of empirical data, using the cement of reasoning and imagination, so as to generate a novel structure of what might be termed an augmented reality. This augmented reality first places readers as close as possible to the experience of the protagonists and then draws them into the counter-investigative work of the sociologist.

But, in order to craft this masonry, the facts need to be tracked down to the smallest detail. Creative freedom is to some extent restricted by the commitment to truth-telling. Thus, when the text says that the officer thinks you never know with Travellers, and that he believes that his was the fatal shot, it is because during his deposition he states that Travellers represent a difficult community for them and, later, that he was probably the one who killed the man. When the text notes that the father thinks the evacuation of the officer was staged to make it look as if he was injured, and imagines that the shots could have led his oxygen bottles to explode and thus transformed his son into a terrorist, these are points made in one of the interviews. Many more examples could be cited, almost line by line. Similarly, the terms employed in the text reproduce as far as possible the words used by the speakers. The gendarmes call their victim the target (*la cible*), the objective (*l'objectif*), the individual or the man; they say that they want to neutralize (*neutraliser*) him, which means to kill him, and euphemistically talk of handling (*prendre en compte*) his father and his brother when they pin them down and handcuff them. The family uses expressions typically belonging to the language of the Roma to speak of the gendarmes (*schmitts, clistés, cagoulés*), translated here as cops, whose semi-automatic weapons are Tommy guns (*mitraillettes*); the lean-to of the house is named a shed (*cabouin*) or a barn (*grange*). When referring to the Travellers, the public prosecutor alternates the slightly pejorative noun gypsy (*manouche*) and the common phrase travelling people (*gens du voyage*). However, the point is not to incorporate verbal tics, syntax errors or clumsy expressions that would undermine the credibility of the speakers and distract readers. Hence the refusal to use the realist effects of quotation marks and dialogues. Furthermore, it is important to remember that, while interviews do allow access to the words of the speaker, records of depositions are not word-for-word transcriptions but summaries of what the court clerk heard. They thus do not constitute a complete reproduction.

No proper name of any person or, indeed, of any place appears, nor any date. This choice of anonymization arises not only out of ethical concerns to protect the individuals involved or legal considerations to protect the author; both these protections are illusory given that modern search engines make it a simple matter to identify all the details of such an event. Anonymization is used above all as a way to draw out the broader meaning of this death, the conditions of its possibility, the actions of the gendarmes, the practice of judges, the campaign led by the family. Specific though this story is, it nevertheless reveals fundamental features of the state's law-enforcement institutions and of the punitive treatment of Travellers: it is not merely a regrettable incident. One exception is made to this rule of anonymization: the forename of the Traveller. Refusing to consign him to anonymity is a way of respecting the memory of the person who is, ultimately, the only victim of the events that occurred one day in early spring at his parents' farm. The fragile trace of a life cut short. An intimate connection through which, for his family, he lives on.

But the plan to render an account of the case in all its complexity soon came up against a major dilemma with regard to the different versions. The problem is the difficulty of recounting the events in an even-handed way. The separate accounts, each one written from a subjective point of view, seek to reconstruct how each person experienced the scene, the events that preceded it and those that followed. This approach inevitably results in the presentation of some experiences that were actually lived and others that were falsified. For whatever one decides about who is telling the truth, the two versions presented, that of the relatives and that of the gendarmes, are irreconcilable. One of them at least is mistaken, and possibly even deliberately false. In order to get as close as possible to subjectivities, experiences should therefore be recounted as they were supposed to have really been lived, including the awareness of deceit, even if this version is radically different from what the individuals concerned said in interviews or depositions. Which effectively would come down to no longer respecting the accounts of the protagonists, introducing from the outset the perspective of an external observer assumed to know what did happen. This is not strictly speaking a moral dilemma, in the sense of choosing the side one thinks speaks the truth (assuming that there is one side that holds this truth). It is simply the logical conundrum of having to reconstruct a scene as if the protagonists had indeed experienced it in the way they tell it, even when they are deliberately misleading their interlocutors. And this has to be done without being able, and without wishing, to decide in advance which of them are telling the truth.

The way out of this dilemma adopted by the sociologist was as follows. In the first stage, he worked on the assumption that all the protagonists were telling the truth, and therefore he adopted their point of view on the basis of the versions they gave. The parallel accounts of the first officer and the father, the second officer and the mother, as reconstructed, are based strictly on the information each of these individuals presented as the truth. This obviously results in entirely incompatible stories. The judicial system chose between them. The public prosecutor in his early statement, and the examining magistrate in her decision, came down in favor of the officers and against the family. The investigation might end there, and this is indeed what almost always happens. But we can also take into consideration the fact that, in the judiciary, not all individuals are treated equally, and not all words are given equal weight, particularly when law-enforcement officers are accused, and also when either the plaintiffs or the accused are Travellers. In the second stage, the sociologist therefore attempted to re-examine the different versions, this time in order to decide whether there were reasons to think that some of them were more consistent than others. He first presented a general discussion of the principles underlying the search for truth and the detection of lies. He then analyzed the different versions, both by drawing out any internal contradictions and improbabilities and by comparing them with the set of external evidence from other testimonies, expert opinions and technical reports. This process resulted in another possible reading of the facts of the case.

In short, the initial intention to give even-handed treatment to the versions of the officers and the family, respecting both equally, did not prevent the subsequent rigorous dissection of the legal arguments and verdict and the presentation of a version based on rational grounds of probability. To venture a parallel from cinema, we might say that the book begins in the manner of *Rashōmon* and ends in the spirit of *Twelve Angry Men*. And this two-stage process is in fact not unlike the construction of the object of study itself, a criminal case. Indeed, the judicial procedure first produces depositions, which are more or less divergent versions of the facts, then an investigation, which examines all the evidence gathered, and finally conclusions. The method followed by the sociologist, right through to the writing-up of his work, ultimately follows a similar pattern. Hence some repetitions, mirroring the process of the counter-investigation. This process might be called a sociological investigation, in reference to but in contrast with the criminal investigation, because it is not limited to the individuals questioned but expands its interrogation to the social conditions of possibility of the events concerned.

As many studies, in France and elsewhere, have established, decisions taken by the courts reflect the balance of power and relations of inequality within a society, which come into play not only in the way certain people are convicted and others acquitted but also in the way social worlds are represented – in this case, those of the gendarmes and of the Travellers. In other words, they involve the production both of justice and of truth. When the sociologist embarked on this project, he knew that he would obviously have no impact on the former, but he thought he might be able to unravel its connection with the latter while the justice system represents the truth of the courts as the sole legitimate one. His counter-investigation could indeed reveal a different reading of the facts. The point was not to take the side of the vanquished against the victors, as historians sometimes put it – in other words to deem the family's version more truthful than that of the officers – but to produce an account independent of all institutional links, of all professional affinities and, as far as possible, of any prejudice. The account must derive purely from the application of a dual principle: all voices deserve the same degree of attention, and the conclusions must proceed purely from the correlation of the available evidence interpreted in context.

It was this dual principle that, in the family's view, the judges had not respected. For the aim of their campaign was not so much to see the officers who fired the fatal shots convicted, though they believed they should be punished in line with what they saw as their level of culpability, as to at last get what they felt was a true account of the conditions in which their son and brother died. An account which, as they put it, would make it possible to raise questions about the police's methods of intervention, the functioning of the penal system, the political context of law and order, and the social representations of Travellers that, taken together, had made his tragic death seemingly ineluctable.

But, for the sociologist, the reason it made sense to engage in this work went beyond the mere critique of punitive practices to which he had devoted his previous books. By focusing on the events that led to the death of the young man, by granting the accounts of his family equal value with those of the gendarmes, by formulating a version independent of that of the courts, by offering a glimpse of what his life had been like, troubled to be sure, but so different from the defamatory portraits painted by the criminal investigation file and the media reconstructions, by pulling him out of oblivion and freeing him from stereotypes, the sociologist thought that it might be possible to return to him, whatever his criminal past, something of what society refuses Travellers, and that the family, through their campaign for justice and truth, had never stopped demanding: respectability.

He started writing.

I

The Father

He is on the doorstep when he sees the gate open and gendarmes, dressed in dark uniforms, balaclavas and helmets, and armed to the teeth, storm into the courtyard. He just has time to say to his son, who is sitting in the little lounge: Go hide, go hide, pointing to the shed. This space, a lean-to around twenty square yards attached to the house, is used as a lumber room. It is where he stores the objects he collects to sell in second-hand markets. Books of cartoons, old furniture, bicycles, strollers. There is also an air conditioner and a generator. Angelo slips behind him, enters the dark room and shuts the door. The father sees him disappear, in his sweatpants and colored tee-shirt.

The GIGN men swarm into the courtyard. A lot of them. Fifteen or so, maybe more. They yell orders. The father sees one of them rush towards him, shouting at him to kneel down with his hands above his head. He refuses to comply. He has never been willing to bow down to the police. The officer pushes him to the ground and makes him lie face down. He handcuffs him behind his back. He trains his Tommy gun on his head. Don't move or we'll shoot. With his tube in his nose, the father says he can't breathe. He is sick, he needs his oxygen. The gendarme will have none of it. Shut up. Struggling to breathe, the old man nevertheless continues to demand, to protest, to curse. There are three disabled people here, he says angrily. His words evidently leave the gendarmes unmoved. A short distance away his wife, who is sick, is kneeling on the ground in front of the caravan, next to their daughter-in-law whom a GIGN man has just brought in, pulling her by the arm. At the side of the house, near the smoking barbecue, his younger son and his brother-in-law are, like him, lying flat on the asphalt with a boot planted in their backs. Standing beside them, gendarmes point the barrel of their weapons at them.

The others have entered the two buildings on the farm where the family live. If they find a door closed they kick it open. They can be heard overturning furniture, throwing objects across the rooms. When they have finished with the houses, the caravans are searched in the same way. After several minutes of this crashing about, the gendarmes come back out to them, clearly annoyed. They have not found the one they are looking for. Where is he? Where is the fugitive? they roar. The parents reply that they have no idea. What do they imagine? That they will give him up to them? All at once, however, the father realizes that it would have been better to answer, to tell them he had gone off into the woods. They might have followed this false trail. He is sorry that he did not think of this in the moment. But it is too late to go back on his words. In any case, the GIGN men have now gathered in the middle of the courtyard. They are talking among themselves in low voices. They seem to be preparing to leave. If only.

A noise in the shed. Angelo must have knocked something down. He must have thought they had all left and wanted to move. A dull thud. But the gendarmes have heard it. Two of them advance with caution, followed by three others. They hold their Tommy guns in their hands. The father tenses on the hard surface of the terrace. He would like to shout to his boy: Give yourself up! But he thinks that is what he will do. He won't play the hero. It's not his style. The GIGN men shove the door open with a crash. They go in. Almost immediately, a burst of gunfire.

They empty their cartridge clips. Then a rattle. Then nothing. His son had no firearm. It can't be him that fired. So it was the cops. Without a word of warning. Lying five yards away from the entrance to the annex, the father is sure. He has heard nothing. Except shots. Followed by a brief moan. And the shout of a gendarme, in the garden, running toward the shed: Hold fire! Stun-grenade him! Now silence. Oppressive. What has happened to his boy? Why aren't they bringing him out if they have captured him? Why do the gendarmes keep coming and going and whispering conspiratorially among themselves? Why aren't they telling them anything? What are they hiding?

One of them appears at the entrance to the lumber room. He is holding a cloth covered in blood. The father thinks he recognizes Angelo's tee-shirt. He cries out: They've killed my boy! A gendarme orders him to be quiet. Hearing the terrible news, the brother, a little further away, rises with a howl of despair. A kick in the back throws him to the ground. The gendarme's combat boot holds him down, head under the barbecue. He protests vociferously. To no avail.

Then something strange happens. Two men come out of the shed, struggling to carry a third, who appears unconscious, his uniform covered with dust. As they pass they knock into the dining table, which falls heavily on the father. It does not seem deliberate, but they don't apologize. They bring their colleague to the middle of the courtyard, take off his vest and helmet, bustle around him for a few minutes. Then the officer, still wearing his balaclava, gets up without effort. He seems to be joking with the others. The father thinks it all looks staged. They want to make it look as if the guy was injured and lost consciousness.

But why did they empty their clip without trying to arrest his son? He wasn't armed, he is sure of that. The hunting rifle is not in the lean-to. Sure, he had a knife in his pocket, like all Travellers, but there's no way he would attack GIGN men with that. An incongruous thought occurs to him. His oxygen bottle. It's somewhere in the barn. When the gendarmes shot in the dark, they could have hit it and caused it to explode. They would certainly have died. Afterwards, they would have said that his son was carrying a bomb, that he was a terrorist. But the idea does not make him smile.

Before long the dance of the emergency services begins. Sirens, trucks. First the firefighters and then the doctor who arrive and then leave again almost immediately. Without Angelo. A bad sign. Although they have still not been told anything, the father is more and more convinced that his son has been killed. Put down like a dog. Murdered, he will say later to the public prosecutor. After a while, their mission accomplished, the cops leave. Without a word of explanation or apology to the parents.

They let their colleagues from the local gendarmerie take over. These men know the family well. They have already had dealings with several of them. For misdemeanors. They've always got on fine. The father knows that you can talk with them. He tries to get some information about what happened in the shed. The gendarmes say they don't know, they weren't there, they were only called to keep an eye on them. They seem to be telling the truth. They, at least, agree to let him sit on a chair and give him his oxygen. Then they take the three men, still handcuffed, and the two women to the garden wall, under the walnut tree. They line them up there. The father says, to provoke them, that you'd think they were in Germany during the war.

After some time, two plain-clothes detectives come and ask him to go to the gendarmerie to make a statement. He refuses to leave until they give them news of his son. Later the mayor comes in person to try and persuade him to go. He gives him the same response. Finally, the public prosecutor himself has to come. Worn down, the father gives in and agrees to go with his family, escorted by the local gendarmes, to the nearby city. There, the criminal investigation officers take their deposition. Without any consideration for the traumatic events they have just lived through. As if they themselves were suspects. They are, indeed, warned that they could be considered accomplices of the fugitive if it turns out they hid him. The father clumsily denies knowing that his son was at his house. He says that he had recently spoken to him on the phone and advised him to return to prison. He wants to talk about what just happened, the way they were treated, the series of events in the lumber room, but the officers keep asking him questions about his boy, his escape, his visits. At this point he refuses to reply and stops the interview. He has still been told nothing about what has happened to Angelo. It is only after this final ordeal that the public prosecutor tells the parents what they had long since guessed: their boy is dead. He also tells them that they cannot return home until the following evening, so as to allow the investigation to proceed. But he gives them permission to go back to pick up what they need for the night.

On the way back, Angelo's family notes that there is now a heavy police presence on the roads into the village, and even beyond. So as to prevent any disturbance, said the public prosecutor. When they arrive at their home, they find gendarmes armed with assault rifles guarding the gate, in the courtyard, in front of the lumber room, the entrance to which is now covered by a white sheet. Cops dog their every step. Houses and caravans are upside down. Doors have been torn away, including those of an inherited wardrobe, which hang off dismally. Amid the chaos, it is difficult to find the oxygen bottles. They kill, rages the father, and on top of that, they think they can do whatever they like.

II

The First Officer

He comes out of the caravan that he has just been searching on his own. Without result, like the two others he has inspected. In the courtyard, three men and two women who have been held by his colleagues are now under guard. The men, lying on the ground, are handcuffed. The women, kneeling, are not. They're not easy, these people. They moan, they complain, they hurl abuse at you. Turning his head, the officer sees two of his comrades go into a lean-to attached to the main building of the farmhouse. They shout out that they have found the target.

An individual belonging to the travelling community who has absconded. Dangerous, they were told during the briefing for the operation. He may have a firearm. The officer even remembers talk about use of hard drugs. Specifically cocaine. This potential risk was the official justification for calling in the GIGN, because initially it was the gendarmerie's surveillance and intervention team responsible for tracking the objective's movements that was supposed to deal with arresting him. But, with gypsies, you never know. The target was therefore pinpointed using geolocation. They were informed that the man had gone to visit his parents that day. The decision was therefore taken to arrest him at his home. They were shown a slide with a map of the site and given the planned outline of the intervention. It consists of taking the family by surprise at lunch time. Eight men are to enter the buildings, three are to take on the caravans, three others are to be positioned in the courtyard, as support, and a final four are to take up position around the low wall of the premises to avoid risk of flight. There are also the commissioned officers, who will stay a little behind. The officer is in the caravan team. Like his colleagues, he is protected by a heavy bullet-proof vest and wears a helmet with a reinforced visor over his balaclava. He is armed with a semi-automatic pistol with three clips of fifteen cartridges each, a pump-action shot-gun, and a small battering ram in case they need to force entry. He also has four stun grenades, a smoke grenade and a flare. The full panoply.

The operation has gone according to plan. At least to begin with. Shortly after midday, the major received confirmation that the fugitive had just arrived at his parents' house. Surrounding access routes were blocked by local gendarmerie units. The little property, situated at the end of the village, was approached discreetly. The GIGN men arrived hidden in the back of an unmarked truck. When they reached the edge of the farm they were told that a car in which the objective might be located was parked in front of the gate. Passing by it, the driver observed that it was indeed the vehicle they had been told about, but not the individual they were seeking. Two of the gendarmes jumped out to question the youth sitting in the car, who had not heard their approach because he was wearing headphones. While others took up position at the four corners of the property, the remainder of the group formed up into assault columns ready to enter the premises, each made up of three men, the first carrying a shield.

The incursion into the courtyard produced the intended effect of surprise. A gendarme shouted: Police! Everybody on the ground, hands on your heads! Several others ran toward the people present in the courtyard. Two men standing by a barbecue, another older man in front of the main building, a woman near the caravan, and a child. During this time the officer, with two of his colleagues, first entered a big barn and then investigated two caravans. Nobody. They were then called toward one of the houses. Still no trace of the target. When he returned to the center of the courtyard, the officer noticed that there was now a young woman among the adults being held under guard. He then entered a third caravan. It took him virtually no time to search the tiny space. The target was not hidden there either.

It is as he comes out into the courtyard that he sees his two comrades enter a small annex and hears them call that they have found the target. He rushes in after them. As soon as he enters the lumber room he sees, by the laser light held by one of his colleagues, a bare-chested man crouched in the darkness, back to the wall, silent, facing them as they are pointing their guns at him. He hears one of them shout that the target has a knife and order him to drop it, but he does not see the weapon himself. His two comrades move back to avoid being stabbed. Another, who entered the lean-to a little before him, pulls out his taser and fires. The electric shock briefly immobilizes the individual, who nevertheless gets up, pulls the wires out with his left hand and throws himself at the two GIGN men opposite him. There is a round of gunfire. Then another round. The officer cannot make out what has just happened. He figures out that one of his teammates has been thrown to the ground and he hears a voice shouting: I'm hit! He thinks his colleague has taken a stray bullet. Probably a friendly-fire shot, as sometimes happens. The man continues to advance, silent, threatening, his right arm raised. He rushes toward one of the gendarmes opposite him. Pushes him up against the wall. Tries to hit him. He now walks toward the officer who, despite the short distance between them, has still not seen the knife but assumes the individual carries one. He reacts immediately. He fires to stop him. Without warning. A single bullet. At short distance. Into the solar plexus. He sees blood flowing over the abdomen. The individual takes one more step, then collapses, head first, onto a bicycle.

The officer puts away his weapon. The room is plunged into darkness once again, except for the wide beam of light coming from the entrance, which is partly blocked by his colleagues. He glimpses the body lying at his feet. He leans down. The individual seems to be in bad shape. He is barely breathing. He gives a weak groan. With the help of his comrade, who a moment before was being threatened with the knife, the officer turns him over and handcuffs him. The aim of the intervention was to arrest him. Job done. When he has finished handcuffing him, he thinks that the guy is all the same not far from dead.

Once the premises have been secured, the officer calls over the radio to say that they had to open fire and that there are two people injured, his teammate and the objective. The emergency services need to be called. His colleague who fired first seems stunned after his fall and is taken outside by two other gendarmes. But the man who is dying receives no care. He was the target. He has been neutralized. He lies, handcuffed, now rendered harmless. With the help of the gendarme still with him at the scene, the officer turns him onto his back. He feels this position is more dignified. His colleague stays beside the man, merely repeating his name softly to check if he reacts. But it is too late. The man no longer has a pulse. He has just succumbed to his injuries. The officer then removes the handcuffs.

The major enters. He calls his men together for a debriefing in the lean-to. He runs over the events that have just taken place with them. He asks each of them for the weapon he used. The officer counts the cartridges left in his clip. Fourteen. So he has used only one bullet. He goes out of the lumber room. He is dazzled by the bright daylight. In the middle of the courtyard, he sees the colleague who has just been brought out. He learns that he is not injured. He was simply in shock.

The emergency services arrive quickly. The firefighters are there first; they realize that there is nothing more they can do. Then comes the doctor from the mobile emergency service, who merely confirms death. Later the forensic team, to collect evidence, and gendarmes from the local brigade, who are responsible for investigation in the immediate aftermath of such incidents. The courtyard has gradually filled up. The GIGN men posted around the property have been joined by colleagues from nearby units. The commander calls the five men who were in the annex together. He asks them to detail the sequence of events once again. Then they find themselves alone together. They ask each other questions, offer comments. Still dazed by what has happened, the officer says little. It is beginning to dawn on him that he and his colleagues have just killed a man.

In his mind he rehearses the arguments he will have to put forward in his deposition. An individual described as dangerous and armed with a gun. His comrade shouting that he has a knife, while another is violently thrown to the floor and he himself is threatened by the man rushing toward him. Therefore legitimate self-defense. The taser shot that only got him more agitated. Hence the need to move to a higher level and use a lethal weapon. It was consequently a case of absolute necessity, and the response can be described as gradual and proportionate. He knows the rules of engagement specified in the Internal Security Code. Priority must be given to negotiation with withdrawal and, if this fails, only fire in the event that one's life or the life of another is in danger. He had no choice, he had to protect his colleague and protect himself. He did not have time to give a warning. It is the first time in his career that he has fired a shot. In fifteen years in the gendarmerie. He joined the GIGN eleven months ago. He will no doubt have to justify his actions to his superiors, and probably also in court. Since, he is convinced, it is his shot that caused the death.

III

The Mother

She comes out of the house holding a metal skewer and goes toward the barbecue. Her brother and her younger son are tending the coals, which are glowing. On the grill, sausages and spareribs are already smoking. The gate bursts open with a crash, and men in balaclavas rush in. She recognizes them straightaway. The GIGN. They shout at them to lie down. One of them runs toward her and grabs the utensil out of her hand. He orders her to kneel down, his weapon trained on her. Her husband is pushed violently to the ground by another gendarme, who handcuffs him. He is having difficulty breathing. The two other men of the house suffer the same fate. Two cops hold them to the ground with a boot in their back. Her brother objects that their meat is burning and asks them to turn it over on the grill. She thinks he obviously hasn't understood who he's dealing with. The guy laughs, takes a bottle of water and empties it over the barbecue. Soon the mother is joined by her daughter-in-law, who was hanging laundry behind the building. Another cop drags her by the arm and forces her, too, to her knees. The whole family is now assembled, threatened by Tommy guns. Except for Angelo, who has managed to hide in the lumber room. Let's hope they will not find him.

During this time the gendarmes have rushed toward the buildings and caravans. The mother hears the row of searches inside the homes. She pictures all the damage. You can't treat people and things like that. What are they supposed to have done wrong? What do they want? They have been given no explanation. Only instructions yelled at them. As if they didn't deserve to be talked to normally. Like human beings. Her position is stressful, painful. She complains that her knees hurt. Nobody listens to her. She sees her grandson looking on, dumbstruck, and hears a cop telling him to go inside to bed. She is finding it harder and harder to stay on her knees. She gets angry, rails, curses them. She is told to be quiet. Unable to tolerate her wails any longer, a gendarme eventually seizes her violently by the arm and drags her over to the steps of the caravan. Her daughter-in-law is allowed to sit next to her.

The GIGN men who have finished searching the premises come over to question them. Do they know where her son is? At last, they're telling us what they're looking for, she thinks. Until that point she hadn't realized they had come for him. He is not often at their house. She hadn't even thought they knew he was here that day. When one of the cops comes up to her and asks her, she loses her temper. She was told to shut her mouth before. So she's shutting it now. The gendarmes move away, shrugging their shoulders. She sees them in discussion with their colleagues in the middle of the courtyard. She imagines that they are unsure how to proceed. How has the fugitive managed to escape? they must be wondering. The thought delights her.

It has finally become relatively quiet. She hears something fall in the barn. Her daughter-in-law looks at her. She has also heard it. The cops have turned round. Two of them approach the shed, followed by three more. Weapons in their hands. She can't see how Angelo could get away from them. It's too bad! He'd almost managed it. The door is kicked open. The first two gendarmes move inside, then the other three. She listens out. Silence has fallen in the courtyard. She can't hear any sound from the annex, except for cops tripping over things. She has to admit, the place is really dark and cluttered. A very brief pause. Then bursts of heavy gunfire. Like a submachine gun. No warning. They didn't ask her son to give himself up. They didn't articulate any order before using their weapons. She hears the order shouted by one of the GIGN men, the major maybe, who she sees coming toward the shed: Hold fire! Stun-grenade him!

Silence again. The muffled sound of a call over the radio. Men going in and out of the shed. There is some sort of confabulation inside. At first she is still stunned by the shock of what she fears she has heard. Then she yells questions at the cops passing in front of her. Nobody seems to pay her any attention. Her husband cries out that their son has been killed. She starts shaking. Not possible! Not like that! Alone, cornered, in the dust. She strains to hear sounds from inside the shed that might suggest that Angelo is still alive. Nothing except the gendarmes talking among themselves. Two of them appear in the entrance. They are carrying a third. She looks at them. They stumble as they pass the table, which tips over onto her husband, and they lay their burden down a little further away to take off his gear. She watches the scene. The man gets up, apparently unharmed. She thinks bitterly: That one's not dead, at least.

When she sees people dressed in white arriving a few minutes later, she finds herself hoping. Maybe her son is just wounded. Maybe she'll see him come out on a stretcher to be taken to the hospital. But the new arrivals are no more inclined than the others to answer their desperate questions. They leave without taking anybody, which is not a good sign. Her daughter-in-law seems even more irrationally hopeful than she is. She even begs a gendarme who is passing the caravan to go into the shed to make sure that Angelo isn't alone, without care. But, seeing the commotion in the courtyard, the mother faces the facts. It really is true. They have killed her son. She shouts her rage at the cops. Some of them stop and look at her. She thinks she sees mockery in their eyes. Soon they gather and go toward their truck, replaced by local gendarmes who take the five prisoners to the garden, under the walnut tree.

These gendarmes aren't mean. They also don't say anything, but it's because they don't know anything. They just hold them. On the other side of the low wall around the property, Angelo's son is in a police car, under close guard. He doesn't know what has happened. He calls out to ask how his father is. His family tell him they don't know. He repeats his question. Finally his grandmother says the words they are all dreading: They have killed him. The boy falls silent. Then he asks again, as if he hadn't heard. She says again, louder: They have killed him. He is dumbfounded.

They wait a long time under the big tree. The mother pictures her son as he arrived, a little after midday. He waved to her as he crossed the courtyard, before going to prepare the barbecue. Decked out in dark sweatpants and a green tee-shirt, he was proudly wearing the black hat his father had given him just that morning. He had long been begging him for it. And that very day, he had inherited it. Here, it's yours! Angelo had been overcome by the gift. His father's hat. His mother thinks: He won't have worn it for long.

But why did they call in the GIGN as well? Couldn't they have sent some of the local gendarmes to ask him to hand himself in? Like they had a few months earlier with her other son, who had then gone to give himself up. And if they really had to send their elite corps, once the cops had heard the noise and realized he was hiding in the shed, couldn't they just have ordered him to come out, or thrown in a stun grenade like the one she assumed was their commanding officer had said? Their house had been subjected to a GIGN operation twenty years ago. That time it was for her husband. He had stolen some cheeses from a dairy. He had been taken by surprise and had fired into the air with an old rifle to give himself time to get away. The next day an assault unit had been sent to his home. When he saw the GIGN men he had immediately complied, letting them arrest him without putting up a fight. A little while later, commenting sarcastically on his colleagues' intervention, which he found disproportionate, an officer from the investigation brigade who knew her husband well had said to her: I would have gone alone and told him to come with me. I've no doubt he would have come. He had added: It's all grandstanding, all that. Something one of the GIGN men said when they arrested her husband comes back to her. He's only alive because we were ordered not to shoot, was his stinging remark. She concludes from it that, if gendarmes can be ordered not to shoot, they can also be ordered to shoot.

IV

The Second Officer

He has just taken over from one of his colleagues, who was guarding the oldest of the house's residents. The old man must be the objective's father. He is on the ground, handcuffed. His breathing is labored. He is railing against the police. Four other members of the family are also held under guard. They too keep up a constant stream of invective, curses and abuse toward them. The officer sees a little boy. He must be about three years old. He keeps looking from the adults shackled on the asphalt to the gendarmes trussed up in their gear. He looks stunned. The officer goes up and says to him: Don't stay here, little guy. Go to bed. The kid disappears without a word. In the courtyard, GIGN men are rushing about, in and out of buildings and caravans.

The operation began about fifteen minutes ago. The officer was one of the first to get out to detain the teen sitting in the car parked in front of the house. They were initially told that the target, an individual described as potentially armed and on the run, was in the vehicle. However, as they approached the car, they learned that he had just entered his parents' house. They still had to handle the youth, who had not shown any sign of resistance. All he had done was call out in an attempt to warn his family. But it did not seem that anyone had heard him inside the family home. It was established that he was indeed the objective's son. When the GIGN men asked him to give himself up, he complied, asking them not to hurt him. The officer and his teammate treated him considerately. As a precaution, they put soft handcuffs on him and passed him to another colleague, who had him lie down on the ground. Then they entered the courtyard, where gendarmes had already brought five members of the family – two women and three men – under control without difficulty, while others had begun to search the residences. Apparently without result. The officer offered to take the place of his comrade who was guarding the oldest of their prisoners to let him continue searching the premises.

The guy he is guarding doesn't seem very friendly. A gendarme who has just come out of the building approaches and asks him where his son is. The fellow mutters that he has no idea. The other members of the family are asked the same question. They give the same answer. The target is nowhere to be found, and they obviously cannot depend on these people to help them locate him. The officer sees his teammate come over. Has the shed adjoining the main building been searched already? He replies that he does not know and sees his colleague go toward the lean-to. So as not to let him venture in alone, he joins him, once he has got someone to take over with his prisoner.

He is the first to enter the space, submachine gun in hand. Almost total darkness. The place seems like a lumber room, the floor littered with more or less bulky objects. Since it seems to be a confined space, the officer puts away his large and unwieldy weapon and takes out his semi-automatic pistol, using its laser to light the cluttered room. Then he hears his comrade shout: Police, police! Come out of there! He understands that the objective has been discovered. The man is hidden under a pile of objects. He stands up suddenly right in front of them, bare-chested, in a state of extreme agitation, shouting abuse, waving his arms and trying to bite them. The officer puts his gun away and approaches the man to try to bring him under control unarmed, but his colleague yells a warning to him: Knife, knife! He steps back, takes out his pistol again and holds the man at bay. He asks him to throw down his weapon. Four gendarmes are now in the lean-to, behind him. He sees two successive taser shots hit the individual. One in each side. The only result is that he becomes more aggressive and more uncontrollable. A total raving fit. Roaring, the man brandishes his knife. He makes big circular movements and, throwing himself on the officer's comrade, tries to stab him in the neck, in the narrow gap between helmet and vest. The officer moves toward him, fires a first round aiming at his chest, then feels a blow on the chin but does not know whether it comes from the individual or his comrade. He falls backward. Lifting his head, he lights the scene and sees that the man is still standing, above him, going for his colleague. He just has the time to fire a second time before losing consciousness.

When he recovers, he finds himself outside in the courtyard, lying down, his gear removed. His colleagues are bustling around him. He is carried to the truck, where the senior officers come to ask how he feels. A little later, there is a debriefing with members of the unit. They talk about the operation: they are happy there were no injuries, they remark on the fury of the objective. The officer talks a lot. He notices that, unlike him, his comrade who also fired remains silent. The forensic technicians ask for their gloves, their balaclavas, their pistols. They undergo alcohol and drug tests.

At three forty-five, the two men who fired shots are notified that they are to be taken into custody, the charge sheet indicating that there are plausible reasons for suspecting that they committed assault with use or threat of a weapon, causing death without intention, as the legal language has it. Although the officer was expecting this decision, he is shocked. But he notices that, actually, it officially comes into effect at one o'clock, at the high point of the events, thus nearly three hours earlier. In the gendarmerie of the nearby city where he is questioned by the criminal investigation officer, he is informed of his rights. He asks to see a doctor, who examines him and certifies that he is fit to be held in custody. Later, he asks to be examined by a forensic pathologist to assess the injuries he ascribes to the attack in the lean-to. However, the report notes that the officer complains of tenderness around his chin and pain in his neck but finds no objective signs, specifically no bruising or abrasion in these areas. Just a few grazes on the forearms. No time off sick. Altogether this makes very little firm evidence. But that's not the point. He fired, he will say in his deposition, to save his colleague's life. He had no choice.

This operation was his second in twenty-four hours. The previous one was the night before. An arrest in a drug-dealing case, with the seizure of a good quantity of product into the bargain. He had gone to bed in the early hours and had been woken around ten for the operation concerning the fugitive. That's how it goes in their job. You have to be ready for action twenty-four seven. Operations can come one after the other. Truth to tell, he doesn't even feel tired. He's used to this rhythm. Eighteen years as a gendarme, half of that time in the GIGN. Eight years overseas. He's served as a paratrooper, a speedboat pilot, an aircraft gunner, an instructor at France's equatorial forest training camp, is qualified to lead VIP security teams and competent in the use of almost all the weapons available to law enforcement; he is a seasoned gendarme. He has fired before. The first time, in a case of illegal fishing. He fired at several individuals with a pump-action shotgun. The second time, in a case involving illegal gold prospectors. He used a so-called less-lethal hand-held weapon against a gold panner. But, up until today, he has never killed anyone.

V

The Doctor

The emergency care dispatch sheet tells him that a call
has just been received from the gendarmerie regarding a
person with a serious gunshot injury. The dispatcher taking
calls that day has passed the information to the emergency service triage doctor, who, following procedure, has
first contacted the fire service, because they can get to the
site more quickly, and then the mobile emergency unit in
the administrative capital. It is eleven minutes past one.
The doctor immediately sets the emergency procedure in
motion and leaves, accompanied by a nurse and a paramedic. From the hospital to the site where the accident has
occurred takes them around fifteen minutes. At that time
there is little traffic, and, in any case, once they get out
of the city they are driving through countryside up to the
village where the event has taken place.

On arrival, the doctor learns from the firefighters that
there is nothing more to be done and the man has actually
died several minutes before they arrived. He asks them
the victim's name and age and the circumstances of his
death. He also exchanges a few words with the gendarmes
and with the criminal investigation officer who is present.
He makes a note of the information he is given. Then,
accompanied by his two colleagues, he crosses the court-

yard of what looks to be a former farm, where several caravans stand alongside the buildings. He is struck by the number of GIGN agents in riot gear who are occupying the site. He also registers the presence of three men, who are handcuffed and lying on the ground, and two women seated not far off, all under close guard. This must be a major public security operation. He has never found himself amid such a heavy law-enforcement deployment. He does not feel comfortable. The older man and woman are remonstrating with the gendarmes. They are accusing them of having killed their son.

He has been told that the body is in the lumber room located to the right-hand side of the main building, close to the place where the five prisoners are being held. He goes over to the small annex, which is submerged in darkness. The criminal investigation officer is with him. As they enter, the paramedic bumps into a crate that splits open, disgorging its contents. They see potatoes rolling under their feet, adding to the quantity of objects littering the floor. The body is lying across the space. The naked torso is riddled with several bullet holes, from which trickles of blood emerge. Darts, probably from a taser, are still stuck in the skin. The doctor establishes death and then withdraws. He is not supposed to touch the cadaver, because the forensic team will certainly be taking photographs and fingerprints. In this kind of situation, his role is limited to drawing up the death certificate. He fills in the personal data and, next to the address of the parents, adds in brackets no fixed address. He records the date of death but does not specify the time, as he does not know it precisely, and in particular because he suspects that it may subsequently prove to be important. He ticks the box for Medico-Legal Concern, which indicates that the death is suspicious and triggers the intervention of the public prosecutor, who will decide whether an investigation is called for. From the moment he arrived on site up to when he signs the death certificate, the criminal investigation officer has stayed with him almost throughout. Once the

formalities are completed, the doctor chats with the firefighters and gendarmes in the courtyard for a little while
and then leaves with the nurse and the paramedic.

On the way back, in the ambulance, he contacts the
dispatcher to send his data. The dispatcher turns out to
come from the village where the intervention took place
and wants to know what happened. The doctor has few
details to give him. He tells him that he initially thought it
was merely a search operation. He describes the scene and
the security measures. He speaks of the victim, whom he
was not able to examine closely, and adds: The guy wasn't
armed. But he clearly does not want to expand on the
subject. He tells the dispatcher: They came over to me and
told me that discretion in this situation was paramount.
In that moment he does not realize that this conversation,
like all calls to and from the mobile emergency unit, is
being recorded and that, given the circumstances, it will
become important evidence for the inquiry.

It is only when he is summoned a year later for the
judicial investigation that he realizes that what he said in
his radio message could become evidence. His assertion
that the guy was not armed contradicts the declarations
of the five gendarmes who were on site in the lean-to and
challenges the claim of legitimate self-defense from the two
who fired, since all of them described the victim rushing at
them with a knife. These are details that he read in an article in the local newspaper two days after the death of the
fugitive. And the instruction to maintain total discretion
could appear to indicate an attempt by the gendarmerie
or the public prosecutor's office to exert pressure on a
potentially embarrassing witness. During his deposition,
he recalls how the criminal investigation officer stayed
with him all the time. The examining magistrate and the
counsel for the plaintiffs insist that he should say who
told him the guy was not armed and who demanded his
total discretion, putting him in a difficult position. He
mumbles muddled and contradictory responses, sensing
that his questioners are not convinced when he says that

he doesn't remember, that the situation was so intense and stressful that he might have been mistaken, and that asking him to keep quiet about what he had seen and heard must simply mean his attention was being drawn to the sensitive nature of this case, or might even just have been a way of reminding him of his ethical obligation to respect medical confidentiality. At one point, pinned down by the lawyer, he nevertheless has to concede that, if he passed this information to the dispatcher, it definitely means that he heard it. He would surely not have gone so far as to invent it.

In the immediate aftermath, as he returns to the hospital with his two colleagues, the doctor feels troubled. The tense atmosphere, the violent death, the pressure from the police. He likes clinical work, emergency medicine, actions that can save lives, not forensic medicine, death certificates, situations where everything is already lost. He has just got back to his department when he receives another call from the gendarmerie. This time, it is at the request of the criminal investigation officer, who has come to notify the two GIGN men charged with causing the death of the man that they are to be held in custody. The Penal Procedure Code specifies that they must undergo medical examination to confirm they are fit to be held in custody and placed in a holding cell. The doctor fills in the required form – a bureaucratic chore that he cannot legally get out of. Strange all the same that they call on him to draw up this certificate, he thinks, as he returns to his department. Usually they call out a general practitioner from the city to perform this service, not a hospital emergency doctor. In fact, it is the first time he has been called in to write up this form. He does not understand this anomaly.

VI

The Sister

She checks her messages and sees that her sister-in-law has texted her. She does not read the message because she is trying not to let herself be distracted. She is doing some return-to-work training, getting basic skills to help her to find work. She is taking it very seriously. She would like to become a hospital cleaner, and then maybe a nursing assistant. Passing her brother this morning when he arrived at the family home just as she was leaving, she spoke to him proudly of the course she was taking. He congratulated her: That's great. That's real life! She understood him to mean that real life was not the troubled existence he led.

Eventually curiosity gets the better of her. She opens the message: Don't come back to the house. Go fetch the children from school. Ours is full of cops. Distraught, she leaves the training session. Why shouldn't she go home? Are the gendarmes looking for her? She hasn't done anything wrong. But she can't stop herself worrying. Always this apprehension, as soon as there's anything to do with gendarmes. She knows all too well what they're capable of. She calls her sister-in-law, who tells her she can't say anything over the phone. She guesses that she is under guard. She tries to get at least a monosyllabic indication, by listing the members of the family who might have dealings with law enforcement, but receives only negative responses. She doesn't even think to mention Angelo, because she believes he has already left their parents' house. Ten minutes go by. The phone rings. Her mother's number is displayed, but it is her father on the other end. He shouts: They've killed your brother! They've killed your brother! She doesn't understand. Does not want to understand. She asks: Is he in the hospital? He replies: No! They killed him. He's dead. We have to go to the station. The line goes dead suddenly. Probably a cop.

On the way, she prays with all her strength that it is not true, that her father is mistaken, that her brother is only injured. At the top of the street leading to the family house, two agents from the neighboring gendarmerie block her way. She asks them why they have put up the roadblock. They tell her they have no idea. They were called to halt traffic without being given any explanation. She tries another way in, from the other side of the village. This time the police presence is more imposing. Half a dozen heavily armed gendarmes she does not know stand in the middle of the road. Seeing the massive deployment, she realizes that something serious really has happened. But she gets no more information than at the previous roadblock. She bursts out: I know what's going on. You've killed my brother. She adds: And you won't let us through because you're down there arranging things to suit you, like you always do.

She moves away. Wracked with grief, feeling powerless, she bursts into tears at the side of the road. A riot police van driving toward the family house stops beside her. The gendarmes at the roadblock further back probably alerted them to her presence. Through the open window, one of the men inside lowers his mirror sunglasses. He stares at her for a few seconds without saying anything. She sees him smile mockingly. The vehicle moves off again.

More than four hours pass before the public prosecutor allows the young woman to return to her home, but only, she is told, to pick up the few things she needs for the night, since she will not be permitted to stay there. When she finally arrives at the gate, which is guarded by heavily armed men, she meets her parents, who have just come back from giving their statements at the gendarmerie. They tell her that her brother has been killed by the GIGN. She is stunned. She goes into the farm courtyard. It's like a war zone, she thinks to herself. It reminds her of video war games. There are gendarmes with assault guns all over the place. They accompany them into the buildings and the caravans. The rooms are in total chaos, in which each of them tries to find medication, clothes, a toiletry bag.

The young woman had hoped to see her brother's body, but, at the sight of the white tarpaulin covering the entrance to the lean-to, she realizes that she will not be allowed to, especially when she sees the crime scene investigation technician going in and out with sample tubes and all kinds of equipment for analysis. Among the sealed evidence, she recognizes the cellphone belonging to her mother, whose health remains delicate following major surgery and who needs to be able to contact her doctors at all times. She loses her temper, demanding that it be returned to her. The cops realize they'd better compromise. Perhaps they are also thinking that they don't need a second victim on their hands. They return the cellphone to the old woman.

The family leaves again, driving off to the home of some relatives. That is where they will spend the night. On the way, Angelo's sister learns of the circumstances of the tragedy. The gendarmes in assault gear, her parents manhandled like criminals, her brother shot dead without warning. Humiliation and violence. The treatment perennially meted out to Travellers by the police, she thinks. Except that, this time, the intervention ended in homicide. She is devastated. When they arrive at the house of the aunt who is putting them up, cousins are waiting for them. They weep for the dead man. The story of the tragedy is told. They rage at the way the gendarmes killed Angelo, the brutality with which they treated his family, their refusal to let them see his body, the fact that they are without any doubt preparing an account that will exonerate them of responsibility for what she sees as the execution of a man alone, unarmed, facing five heavily equipped and weaponed GIGN men. Legitimate self-defense. Just like every time a Traveller dies under police gunfire.

After a sleepless night, the sister gets up at first light to buy the newspaper. Reading the portrait painted of her brother, who is presented as a dangerous fugitive, and the account of the events that repeats the GIGN's version, so different from that recounted to her by her parents, she feels her anger rising. They have killed her brother. And now, she thinks furiously, they are sullying his memory and acquitting his killers in advance. Later, with her parents, she watches the regional news on television. Extracts from the public prosecutor's press conference are shown. Facing the journalists, he states that a Traveller on the run attacked gendarmes with a knife and that they had no choice but to shoot to protect themselves, after trying without success to subdue him with taser shots. Of course, he concludes, legitimate self-defense will have to be confirmed by the investigation he has set in motion.

The sister is outraged. She feels wounded by what she sees as lies aimed at exonerating the GIGN men in advance, by making her brother solely responsible for his own death. Her parents had been called in to make a statement, but they had not been heard. At no point in the public prosecutor's presentation was there any mention of their version of events, which completely contradicts that of the gendarmes. As for the journalist on the local daily paper who is reporting on the case, he has not bothered to get in touch with them. Thus readers will learn that a potentially dangerous escapee belonging to the travelling community attacked gendarmes who had come to arrest him with a knife, and that, having failed to respond to instructions to give himself up and to taser shots, he had to be killed. A story which no doubt matches up with the public's image of Travellers. Only the regional television correspondent interviewed the younger brother who witnessed the events, giving airtime to an alternative version of the facts. He describes how the gendarmes entered the lean-to and fired only two seconds later.

But the young woman's anger is tempered by anxiety. Why was her brother's body left in the dust, without allowing them to see him, without giving them permission to keep vigil over him? What if they don't give it back to them? The same idea has occurred to her parents, and they are full of fear. Once they have heard the public prosecutor on the television, they feel anything is possible. They talk of other cases where families have not recovered the body of a relative killed by the police. Or, at least, not immediately. Suspicion creeps into their minds. And, also, why are they not being allowed to go home? What are the gendarmes, the investigators and the magistrates doing all this time, in their absence? Everyone is convinced they are arranging the scene of the events and getting the GIGN men's accounts in line so as to make their version credible.

As she waits to be allowed to return home, Angelo's sister tries to tear herself away from these painful thoughts. She returns to the memory of her last meeting with her brother, the previous morning. Giving his nephews a hug, he told them laughingly: You have to work hard at school. One of you will be my lawyer one day. As she parted company with him, she expressed concern as she usually did: Take care of yourself. He replied calmly: Don't worry. You run as long as you can. It's the last thing he said to me, thinks the young woman, suddenly moved to tears, and a few hours later I find out that he is dead without having run. Trapped like a rat, in the corner where he had hidden. Dying between four walls, that's exactly what he didn't want.

VII

The Prosecutor

He is in a meeting of the regional council when he receives a call from his collaborator on duty about a shooting incident that has occurred in the course of an intervention by gendarmes at the home of travelling people. It is one fifteen. The man who was to be arrested is seriously injured, and there may be another casualty on the police side. As the public prosecutor makes his way to the location, he remembers what the colleague whom he succeeded told him when he took office. Her abiding memory of her years in the public prosecutor's office was of an episode that had been particularly challenging to manage: the death, a few years earlier, of a young gypsy killed by gendarmes had aroused a powerful reaction from his community, which had, she told him, wreaked havoc in the small town where the incident had occurred. Recalling her words, the public prosecutor realizes that the case he has just been told about is likely to be extremely sensitive. Once on site, he learns further that the man arrested is dead and that, in fact, none of the gendarmes is injured. This news confirms his fears, especially as those he speaks to assert that the officers fired in legitimate self-defense.

Several aspects of this case immediately strike him as out of the ordinary, as he gradually discovers the details. Thus, the presence of investigators from the Research Section of a neighboring département, with an arrest warrant signed by an examining magistrate, is highly unusual in what is ultimately a simple failure to return to prison after home leave. In such cases the problem is usually dealt with at the local level by the sentence enforcement judge. Still more remarkable is the recourse to the GIGN, which suggests an exceptionally dangerous operation. The majority of arrests are carried out by a regional squad, or perhaps, if a degree of risk is predicted, by the gendarmerie's surveillance and intervention team, or more rarely by the gendarmerie's specialist protection team, which is reserved in principle for terrorist attacks. The fact that they went so far as to call on the elite units of the national gendarmerie's intervention group, designed to deal with exceptionally dangerous situations, in order to arrest an individual from the travelling community is a source of astonishment to the public prosecutor. He therefore questions his colleagues in the Research Section, who explain that the man on the run was considered not only dangerous but also determined not to go back to prison, justifying the recourse to these exceptional means. Duly noted.

As he learns how the arrest proceeded, he realizes that the situation is delicate because the decisions he will take will expose him either to the anger of the victim's family or to discontent on the part of law-enforcement agencies, or both. On the one hand, the information about the man's death should not be made public too early, both out of respect for the family, who should be the first to be notified, and to pre-empt any expressions of outrage from travelling people, among whom the memory of the young man killed by a gendarme a few years earlier remains raw, as is clear from the annual marking of the anniversary of his death. It is therefore vital to control the spread of the news. Nothing is said to the parents, and the gendarmes, firefighters and doctor present at the scene are expressly requested not to disclose the facts. On the other hand, all the protagonists need to be asked to give statements as soon after the event as possible, which means that some of the gendarmes should not return to barracks but should have their depositions taken by criminal investigation officers that day; above all, a decision has to be made whether or not to remand in custody those who fired the fatal shots, as this does not automatically follow in such situations.

In this respect, the political context is by no means neutral. Following the 2015 terrorist attacks in Paris, not only has a state of emergency been introduced, giving law-enforcement agents more prerogatives, but also the law has been modified in order to modernize, as official parlance has it – in other words, to extend – the use of their weapons. Given the broadening of what constitutes legitimate self-defense both in the letter of the law and in the mind of judges, placing the officers in custody precisely when they are claiming such legitimate self-defense runs counter to the shift in the legislation and in society itself, which seems to be comfortable with the increased power accorded to the police. After speaking with the national attorney general and the general inspectorate of the gendarmerie, the public prosecutor, who has in the meantime called in a deputy to support him, eventually confirms that he is going to take statements from all the witnesses and to place the two who fired in custody. This creates tension among the members of the GIGN, who expected more leniency from the public prosecutor's office. For the two officers who fired, being held in custody on a charge of assault with use or threat of a weapon leading to involuntary homicide is a heavy blow. They understand that they are being treated as suspects.

For the public prosecutor, however, this move is designed primarily to ensure that statements are taken from the men who fired within the required period and that a re-enactment can be conducted at the scene, while demonstrating to the victim's family that the justice system is taking the case seriously. At the point when these decisions are being made, the parents, who are still under the guard of gendarmes, know nothing of this. Nor do they know what happened in the lean-to. Though they suspect that the GIGN's intervention came to a fatal conclusion, they continue to question the gendarmes about what has happened to their son. But they get not the slightest response. In protest, they declare that they will not agree to give their statements until they have been told. Some hours later the public prosecutor, who has returned to the regional court to organize the next stage of the judicial procedures, receives a call from the commander present at the location, who wearily suggests they be brought in by force. If they put up a fight they will be charged with resisting an officer invested with public authority, he adds. The public prosecutor rejects this solution, which would only fan the flames of what is already a tense situation. He therefore returns to the scene to try to persuade the father, who he senses is respected as the head of the family. He explains to him that he wishes to know what really happened, and who did what. This aim of knowing the truth, he continues, is without doubt one they both share, and, in order to achieve it, the family, who were present during the operation, must be able to say what they experienced, saw, heard. Pretending not to know that the man's son has been killed, he promises, once they have made their statements, to enquire after his health and communicate the information he obtains. The father then gives his assent. He does so on one condition: they will go in their own car, not in a law-enforcement vehicle. Cue further negotiation by the public prosecutor, this time with the commander, to obtain authorization for this non-regulation transport, which eventually, escorted by police motorcyclists, drives to the central offices of the gendarmerie.

When the members of the family have each given their statement, the public prosecutor gathers them together in a small room. He claims he knows gypsies well, because he often deals with them, and he likes them. He knows that this is going to be a difficult time for the victim's family, but he trusts in their reactions. Against the advice of the head of the gendarmerie unit, he therefore refuses to be accompanied by law-enforcement officers so as not to exacerbate tensions that are already raw. Only two gendarmes are present. Five hours after the shooting in the lean-to, the father, the mother, the brother, the sister-in-law, the uncle and the son are finally going to find out what happened there. The public prosecutor starts by telling them that it is always difficult to get to the real truth, but he guarantees that they will work, in transparency and good faith, using all the tools the law provides, to establish what will be called judicial truth. Then comes the delicate moment of what he calls the revelation. He informs them of the death and offers them his condolences. Even though they were expecting this terrible news, the members of the family are both devastated and furious. The son flares up at the public prosecutor, but his grandfather manages to calm him down. The public prosecutor then explains that, because the scene of the tragedy needs to be examined for evidence, they will not be able to go back home, but he gives them permission to go by their house to pick up a few things. Attempting to establish a relation of trust, in an unusual gesture he gives the mother his professional cellphone number so that she can reach him in case of need. As the members of the family get ready to leave, he entreats them to do all they can to avoid disturbances like those that occurred on a similar occasion. He knows, however, that in any case exceptional measures have been implemented, and that the police have taken up position on all the roads around the scene.

During this time, the investigative machinery is being rolled out. First there is the team sent from the General Inspectorate of the Gendarmerie, which deals with taking statements from all the witnesses, including the two charged, and gathers all the materials relating to the case. Then there is the referral to the Research Section for violence against officers invested with public authority, since the gendarmes claim they were attacked before they fired, even though, in view of the death of the presumed perpetrator, the case will obviously be closed without going to court. Finally, there will be the reconstruction of the incident in the presence of a ballistics expert from the gendarmerie's National Institute of Criminal Investigation. This procedure is a sort of re-enactment to determine whether any contradiction or improbability arises in the way the events have been recounted or are replayed. However, the five members of the family who witnessed them will not be included because, in the public prosecutor's view, they saw nothing of interest, since the killing took place in the lumber room. In his opinion, if they say they heard something it is difficult to put much stock in it, because everyone hears what they want to hear. In their absence, the re-enactment is not a real reconstruction. But it means extending the custody of the two who fired, who appear very upset by the shame this decision casts on them.

After this final stage, having read the witness statements, spoken with the ballistics expert and examined the other evidence in the case file, the public prosecutor is firmly convinced that the officers acted in legitimate self-defense, although he admits that the course of events as they recount it is, to say the least, difficult to understand. But the fact that there were eight shots, of which five hit their target, paradoxically seems to him to demonstrate that there was no intention to cause death, as might have been assumed if a single shot had been aimed at the head. He does not give credence to the declarations of the members of the family that the whole thing took only a few seconds, for how could the successive phases described by the officers be fitted into such a short time: the entry into the lean-to, the discovery of the individual, the attempt to seize him unarmed, the attack on the gendarmes with a knife, the repeated instruction to surrender, the two ineffective taser shots, the continuing frenzied attack, the eventual opening of fire? Indeed, since he is convinced the officers are telling the truth, he cannot be equally persuaded that the victim's relatives too are doing so. The gendarmes' version obviously contradicts the family's version. Moreover, while it is clear to him that the GIGN were not prepared for such a situation and used excessive measures in their intervention, they acted as they ought to when confronted with their attacker, attempting to dissuade him from using his weapon and gradually escalating the use of theirs. This interpretation meets all the necessary criteria to demonstrate legitimate self-defense.

In the following few days, once he has communicated the main aspects of the case to the press, the public prosecutor decides to initiate a judicial investigation and, thus, to entrust the case to an examining magistrate. Yet he sees little point in this procedure, not imagining that it could lead to any conclusion different from his own. Hence his surprise when, following her initial questioning of the two who fired the fatal shots, the magistrate places them under formal investigation, implying by this decision that, according to the terms of the law, she believes there are serious and consistent indications of their probable responsibility for the death of the Traveller. The public prosecutor had been expecting her to assign them the more neutral status of assisted witness, which does not imply such suspicion, and thus understands that, through this decision, his colleague is expressing a manifest doubt as to their version of the events. This is confirmed when a few months later he receives a court notification of a visit to the location, which again suggests that the magistrate wishes to conduct some form of reconstruction, this time including the family, who were excluded from the first re-enactment. The main aim of this procedure is to take their claims seriously, by checking what they had been able to see and hear at the time of the killing. But the public prosecutor will never know what the judge would have decided at the end of her judicial investigation, because, in a move to work closer to her home, she is transferred to another jurisdiction before she has written up her final adjudication. It is therefore a different examining magistrate, entirely new to the role and to the position, who is confronted with this delicate case when she arrives and has to deal with it as a matter of urgency without having taken part in the judicial investigation.

With hindsight, the public prosecutor believes that, ultimately, this tragedy comes down to an unfortunate encounter between a guy who was determined, to be sure, but armed only with a knife, and the most highly trained and heavily equipped personnel in the French internal security forces. The two were not evenly matched, he thinks. Extreme measures were chosen without the possibility of bringing them down in line with the circumstances. The officers were unable to adapt to the situation. But why were they brought in? If gendarmes from a regional squad had been called up, would they not have handled it better? The moral of the story, in his view, is that the arrest of a member of the travelling community should have nothing in common with putting a group of terrorists out of action. The problem is that the GIGN seems not to have understood that.

VIII

The Journalist

He gets the headline the next day: Fugitive killed as he is arrested. The phrase runs across the front page of the daily newspaper above a wide-shot photo of a farm building with a truck and two vehicles of the gendarmerie parked in front of them. Below, the journalist writes: The police arrived at the place where the escaped prisoner was located in the early afternoon. The fugitive was known as a determined, potentially dangerous man. Five individuals were initially held. The man, who was in his thirties, was finally located. Several shots were fired in circumstances as yet undetermined, and the man died. A member of the travelling community, the fugitive was known to the courts for his involvement in burglaries with a group of Parisians known as the BMW gang. He had over a dozen convictions, mainly for theft.

The following day the journalist's headline reads: Gendarmes claim they fired in self-defense. Below, he writes: The public prosecutor has gone over the circumstances of the gendarmerie operation that turned into tragedy. The man, who belonged to the travelling community, had been on the run for six months. There was an arrest warrant out for him. He had a long criminal record, mostly for aggravated theft. He was considered potentially dangerous. He had been arrested in possession of weapons several times. For this reason, investigators were assigned the back-up of their colleagues from the regional GIGN branch. The gendarmes entered the former farm where the family of the young gypsy on the run live. Searching for the fugitive, the gendarmes entered a small annex plunged in darkness.

The remainder of the article is a long quote from the public prosecutor: The man was hiding at the back of the annex. The gendarmes asked him to give himself up. He got up, they came toward him, and he then pulled out a knife and brandished it, advancing with threatening circular movements. The gendarmes moved back and used an electric pulse gun. But that failed to have the expected effect, and he managed to pull out one of the darts. This clearly increased his determination not to be arrested, and he rushed a gendarme, attempting to stab him in the face and neck. It was in these circumstances that a first officer used his weapon; then a second did the same, enabling him to neutralize the man. The article is illustrated with a Google Earth screen shot showing a gate, through which a caravan can be glimpsed. It is the parents' farm where the events took place.

The only source for the articles is the public prosecutor, who himself repeats the version given him by the gendarmes. The journalist has not tried to meet with the victim's relatives. Indeed, he never will over the course of the subsequent years. That is not his role. He is not an investigator. His role is to report on the local news and legal cases in the region. These are the subjects that interest the local readership. Stories about murders, sexual predators, women raped, abused children, criminal trials, but also the more humdrum happenings: shoplifting, road traffic accidents, motorbike rodeos, falls from horseback, stubble fires. Everyday life through the lens of major crime and minor incidents. He has his ways into the courts of law, contacts that enable him to stay informed about events almost in real time, and to inform readers in his turn. In his articles on the cases being handled by the justice system, he generally reports what is communicated to him by the public prosecutor's office. Thus, he reiterates the official version, that of the authorities, which hence becomes the authoritative version, since the regional daily paper is the media source of reference for a large proportion of the population. That day, he merely attended the public prosecutor's press conference and faithfully reconstituted its main points.

While he strives to stick to the facts, to avoid analysis and to hold back from making comments, his choices of vocabulary and his narrative construction are not neutral. The man being sought becomes a fugitive, an escaped prisoner. Even though the articles point out that he simply failed to return to prison after home leave, the use of this nominal form reduces the Traveller to a character on the run, making him seem much more disturbing than the reality of a man who often visits his parents, his children and his ex-girlfriend without really hiding. Other, strictly descriptive elements further reinforce the unfavorable impression, since he is said to be potentially dangerous and known to the courts for his participation in burglaries. He has even been arrested in possession of weapons, but it is not pointed out that this was his knife, an object that Travellers are never without. The almost casual note that he belongs to the travelling community adds the weight of prejudice against this group, particularly since the two articles evoke the risk of disorder, as happened a few years earlier, the journalist writes, when incidents broke out following the death of a young gypsy shot by a gendarme. All of these elements are taken from the information provided by the public prosecutor's office, which is faithfully reproduced in the newspaper.

In the second article, published twenty-four hours after the first, the portrait of the deceased has even become more detailed. And darker. It was known that he had over a dozen convictions, mainly for theft. It is now revealed that his long criminal record comprised twenty-one citations, mostly relating to aggravated theft. He was deemed to be potentially dangerous. Now it is reported that he was several times arrested in possession of weapons. Thus, the idea the reader gets of him from these pages makes it plausible that he might have attacked the gendarmes and that their shots were therefore necessary; the fact that he belongs to the travelling community makes this seem all the more likely. Tarnished by the numerous offenses he committed and by the attack he is supposed to have perpetrated in the lean-to, this image leaves little chance that he will be seen as the victim of police violence.

Through little touches, the portrait, which aligns with the actions of which he is accused, becomes imprinted in the minds of the public, who are thus likely to be receptive to the version presented by the public prosecutor. Whereas the first article spoke of shedding light on the circumstances in which the events played out, the second begins with an assertion, albeit still cautious: the hypothesis of legitimate self-defense seems the most likely. But this is preceded by a much more definite headline: Fugitive brandished a knife in attack on gendarmes. The fact that the family vehemently contests this account is not mentioned anywhere. It will be several weeks before it is mentioned in the regional daily, and even then allusively, when another journalist reports on the campaign by the collective formed to demand justice.

IX

Dignity

This is what the family is fighting for. Dignity for Angelo, who they are convinced was killed without reason and without warning. Dignity for his memory, sullied by a public account that they feel is degrading and mendacious. Dignity for his parents, abused, humiliated and treated like criminals during the GIGN operation. More broadly, dignity for Travellers, who are always represented in a negative light, denigrated, belittled, marginalized, seen as second-class citizens.

On the evening of the tragedy, when the public prosecutor greeted the parents, informed them of the death of their son, offered them his condolences, and then immediately added: I hope it's not going to be as it was in 2010, they understood. His greatest concern, they realized, was the risk of disorder, as he put it. He was referring to events that occurred in the region seven years earlier. A twenty-two-year-old Traveller who had fled after robbing a young man of twenty euros he had just withdrawn from an ATM had been killed by a gendarme at a roadblock. In his version, which was initially accepted by the public prosecutor's office, the gendarme said that it was legitimate self-defense, as he was threatened by the vehicle that had refused to stop. The account given by the victim's brother, who was driving the car, spoke of shots fired without warning as he was slowing down. In the hours following the death of the young man, on the village square the gendarmerie had been vandalized, street furniture had been destroyed and several trees had been torn down. This reaction became a major news story and resulted in a heavy police deployment and a series of arrests.

Twelve days later, the French president gave what became known as the Grenoble speech. Fusing together the recent incidents and urban riots that had occurred shortly before, following the police killing of an armed robber, he announced the launch of a war on drug-dealers and criminals, the reinforcement of penal sanctions for perpetrators of violence against officers invested with public authority, the introduction of deprivation of nationality for persons of foreign origin found guilty of such attacks, a clampdown on illegal immigration, and the demolition of unauthorized Roma camps. The president thus added a supposed Roma question to the already well-worn association of criminality with immigration. The speech marked the starting point of a new security policy, and among its results was the deportation of thousands of Roma from France. The expulsion operation was immediately condemned by the European Commission, the United Nations, and even the Pope. In the view of many, then, the events of 2010 served as a pretext for renewed stigmatization and repression of Travellers in France. The public prosecutor's reference to these events, in the form of a barely veiled warning, could not fail to hit home with the parents he had just informed of the death of their son.

When she hears her father and mother repeat the public prosecutor's remark, the sister is angry. The automatic association of Travellers with violence wounds her. Is it not the gendarmes who are the source of the violence? she wonders. Not just the violence that killed her brother but also the violence to which her family were subjected. And, more broadly, the violence of the very principle of the GIGN operation, as if the arrest of a Traveller accused of what

were, after all, only misdemeanors required deployment
of the kind of exceptional measures usually reserved for
terrorist attacks and hostage situations. The public prosecutor's warning, and what it reveals about the way the
authorities see them, acts as a wake-up call. We mustn't
fall into their trap, thinks Angelo's sister. We must not
fall into that pattern, which works to the authorities'
advantage because afterwards people do not talk about
the person who was killed, only about the incidents that
followed. They must not be able to say: Look how these
people behave, we told you so. It's true, she admits, that,
in the moment, you feel so angry at such injustice that you
want to rebel. But that reaction would immediately be
taken up to justify repression of their community. What's
more, it's important not to choose the wrong target, burning the cars and breaking the shop windows of people who
have nothing to do with the events. After her brother died,
some people wanted to go out smashing things up, but she
dissuaded them. It would only confirm people's prejudices,
she told them – their scorn and their fear of Travellers.

It is that scorn and fear that lead to their being relegated
to the fringes of society. Undesirable and dreaded. They
all know it. There is a sign you can't mistake. When they
arrive in a town or a village they don't know, if they don't
find directions to a reception ground for travelling people,
which is the official term for the sites reserved for them,
they look for signposts to the trash dump or the sewage
works. It is always there that they are allowed to set up
camp. With the rejects or the pollution. Far from view,
close to the garbage. Who bothers about what is signi-
fied by this consignment to places that are physically and
symbolically contaminated? Who wonders how Travellers
might feel, finding themselves thus confined to abject and
unsanitary spaces? And even then they're still waiting for
full enactment of the law of 5 July 2000, which requires
that towns with more than 5,000 inhabitants, and those
villages designated in the *département*'s urban planning,
create such spaces. Twenty years after that legislation was

voted through, and despite financial incentives from public authorities and sanctions laid down but rarely applied against councils that fail to meet their obligations, only two-thirds of the planned sites have been provided nationwide, and the level falls to ten to fifteen percent in the wealthier areas.

The rejection of Travellers is thus evident both in their almost total exclusion from some places, in contravention of a law that is only half-heartedly applied, and in their relegation in many others, which follow the letter of the law but barely tolerate them. At the same time the chronic shortage of sites leads them to occupy land without authorization, resulting in their becoming further stigmatized by the general population, more harshly repressed by the authorities, and more exposed to precarity. Angelo's father and mother have long avoided these *platz*, the Romani term for reception sites, because they are often inconvenient and overcrowded, and they also offer no real possibility of gathering the members of one family together because of the administrative formalities imposed. In order to be together, they first settled on a piece of land belonging to the father's parents and then, when they died, on the farm that belonged to the mother's parents. That is where their son was killed.

The day after the tragedy, when they return to the family home exhausted, overwhelmed, defeated, they decide not to let the matter rest. They say to one another that they cannot allow the lies they have read and heard to be repeated and believed. They have to do something. Angelo's father wants to file a complaint. But going to the gendarmerie to accuse the gendarmes of murder? Them, Travellers, demanding justice for one of their own, presented as a repeat criminal, killed when he had escaped from prison, and having allegedly attacked the gendarmes who had come to arrest him? Who would listen to them? Would their complaint even be recorded? That fight is lost before it starts. And in any case the public prosecutor has told the press that he has initiated an investigation.

So they have to wait. Even though it is hard to believe in the impartiality of such an investigation, there's not much more they can do from a legal point of view. All the same, they think, they can't just do nothing.

It is Angelo's sister who takes the initiative. In her caravan, she records a seven-minute statement to camera, addressed to a virtual audience without yet knowing what she will do with it. I'm speaking in my own words, she explains. We are who we are. But we are not animals. We have the right to the truth. Both distraught and angry, she contests the version presented by the public prosecutor on television, reminding him that he has simply forgotten to mention the presence at the scene of five members of Angelo's family, who testify to a very different course of events. They maintain that they heard nothing before the fatal gunshots, that there were neither sounds suggestive of a fight nor shouts instructing him to give himself up. The gendarmes cornered her brother like a rat in the barn where he took refuge. In her view, it was an execution. There is no other word for it. Because you don't send GIGN commandos to arrest someone like him. You do that for really dangerous people. So, she gives a warning. Every time gendarmes or police kill gypsies or Arabs, you see the same manipulations of the truth. But that can't go on. This time, they will not take it lying down. This must stop, this must stop, she repeats, with emotion. A little while later, she shows the video to her father, who tells her she must publish it. A cousin posts it on YouTube. In the following days, the recording circulates around local and even national activist networks on social media.

A few hours later, she is contacted by the founder of a collective set up to combat police violence. This woman's brother, Amine, was also killed by law-enforcement agents. He was also a repeat criminal, and he also had been sought as an escapee because he had not returned from home leave. Initially, the police officer who shot him had been acquitted on grounds of legitimate self-defense, despite the fact that the fatal shot had hit the victim in

the back. On appeal, the verdict was overturned after
the officer's colleague, the only witness, admitted that
he had lied. The officer was therefore sentenced to five
years' suspension and forbidden to carry a weapon during
that time. The indictment was for intentional violence
leading to involuntary homicide, a crime punishable by
a maximum of fifteen years' imprisonment. The same as
the charge against the two officers who fired at Angelo.
The sentence was of course exceptionally light compared
to what the officer could have received, but it was at
least the beginning of recognition that there are limits to
the impunity generally enjoyed by the police. The appeal
court case had taken place only three weeks before the
events in the lean-to, and it is thus still in the wake of
her response to this rare court verdict against a police
officer that Amine's sister calls Angelo's sister. To share
her experience with her. To encourage her to stand up
for her rights. To suggest that she press charges as a civil
party to the criminal case. To explain that this procedure
does not mean they have to go to the gendarmerie. She
gives her the contact details for her lawyer. Two days
later, the sister and her younger brother go to Paris and
meet the counsel, who agrees to take on their case. I'm not
here to sell you a dream, she warns them. In these cases,
it's David versus Goliath, she adds. But she is touched by
Angelo's case. She tells them so. They understand that it
will not be just another case for her. They feel, for once,
that someone is taking them into consideration. She acted
human with us, they say to each other as they leave the
meeting.

Over the next days, support flows in. Meetings take
place. They think about the best response to the judicial
and media machine that has already established its version
of the facts. Someone suggests they organize a march.
Nobody in the family had thought of it. Indeed, it is not
in the repertoire of practices of their travelling community.
But it seems like a good idea. A way of disproving the
public prosecutor's fears of disorder and showing how

unnecessary the police deployment around their house was. Let's not respond to violence with violence, thinks Angelo's sister. We have to do something Travellers have never done before. We'll march.

X

Campaign

It began as soon the video was put up online. It circulated on social media, quickly reposted by a Roma community organization and by families who had also lost a relative during interactions with law-enforcement agents. A collection was set up almost immediately. The money raised enabled them to pay the one-thousand-five-hundred-euro required to initiate the procedure for filing a complaint. It was also thanks to this fund that they were able to pay the three-thousand-euro funeral costs. Taking care of these practical, primarily financial issues is crucial in such campaigns against police violence, which almost always involve people of modest income. Local activists coming from the fight against racism and discrimination, the alter-globalization movement, and the radical left are actively involved in this solidarity.

Within a few days, a collective forms, few in number, but effective. Seeking ways to take action non-violently. Respectful of the legal context, particularly the fact that a judicial procedure is under way at the same time, a procedure in whose independence they want to believe. And above all respectful of the wishes of the family, in light of the painful experience of a recent campaign to expose the circumstances surrounding the death of a young man of African origin killed by the police, which was brought to an end after the authorities put pressure on his family. A collaborative website that disseminates local news by quoting the words of the people concerned without the usual journalistic filter, part of a national alternative media network, plays an important role. First, by transcribing extracts from the sister's video four days after it is posted. Then, a week after the tragedy, by posting an article that presents a different version from that published in the regional press. And, finally, by publicizing the first gathering in Angelo's memory, which is held outside the criminal court less than a month after the events. A gathering to demand justice and truth.

The demonstration is announced. It draws two hundred people, maybe more. Mainly people from the region but also representatives of collectives calling for justice and truth for other victims of the police, from all over the country. There are also members of Angelo's extended family. Not many, but everyone knows that demonstrating is not part of Travellers' habitual repertoire of protest actions. Among those who have come, some would have liked a more direct confrontation with law-enforcement institutions, which are held responsible as a whole for all the tragedies in which Travellers have recently lost their lives. Yet the units present to monitor the event remain discreet, almost invisible, avoiding all provocation. A regional intelligence officer and a few municipal constables observe the scene from afar. Large numbers of police and gendarmerie reinforcements stand ready some distance away, within and around the city, prepared to intervene.

But everything goes well. Angelo's sister speaks, as does a man almost one hundred years old, seen as a hero of the Roma community because he escaped Nazi concentration camps and fought with the Resistance during World War II. Not long after the demonstration, it is featured on the front page of the local daily paper, with a long article inside. For the first time the family are interviewed and are able to talk about their legal challenge to the GIGN operation. The author of the article adds a human touch to her account of the event as she describes Angelo's younger son shouting through a megaphone: No justice, no peace!, and breaking off in tears. From the organizers' point of view, it is successful on three levels. Because the campaign means that the tragedy can be spoken of in terms other than those of the official version put out by the public prosecutor's office. Because such a peaceful protest following the death of one of their community is virtually a first in the history of Travellers. Above all because the fact that the event was peaceful and dignified is publicly acknowleged, and these words are rarely associated with the travelling community.

Following this first successful action, the collective is keen to keep up the pressure to have its demand for justice and truth heard. But it is small and receives little support. On the one hand, the number of really active members, almost all women, is barely half a dozen, though they are regularly joined by tens of others when events are organized. On the other hand, at the local level, councils, parties, unions and even campaigning organizations are, with few exceptions, reluctant to back a cause involving Travellers. Despite these obstacles, the campaign keeps going, careful to avoid any disorder that might discredit the community and shift the debate from police brutality to the disturbances provoked by it.

From the moment when she recorded the video that sparked the movement, Angelo's sister made a point of linking the tragedy she had just experienced to other cases where youths and men had died during the course of interactions with the police in low-income neighborhoods. She pointed out that the victims always belonged to ethnic or racial minorities and that, ultimately, above and beyond their differences, those who were campaigning in defense of their memory shared the same experience of the police and the justice system. When the campaign got under way, this broadening of the cause immediately became a fact. Links were established with other families. The family of

Lamine Dieng, a twenty-five-year-old man who died in Paris in a police vehicle following a violent arrest during which he was handcuffed, held face down on the ground and immobilized using a technique considered dangerous; the ruling dismissing the case was confirmed on appeal ten years after the event. The family of Wissam El-Yamni, a thirty-year-old man arrested in Clermont-Ferrand for throwing a stone at a police vehicle, who was beaten by officers, fell into a coma at the station, and died nine days later from a cardiac arrest brought on by being held in a stress position known as folding; seven years later, there was still no court ruling on the case. The family of Adama Traoré, a twenty-four-year-old man arrested in Beaumont-sur-Oise, found dead a few hours later in the gendarmerie as a consequence, according to independent medical expert reports, of suffocation linked to being held face down on the ground; three years later the case was still under investigation with contradictory assessments by official coroners.

What these stories, and many others, have in common is the delay in informing the family of the death, sometimes also in returning the body to them, the public prosecutor's immediate acceptance of the version of the police, often supported by medical reports exonerating them, and the long-drawn-out judicial procedure, generally ending with a dismissal of the case and the exoneration of the officers charged. But what distinguishes these families from many others similarly bereaved is the energy they, often the sisters of victims, have invested in their demand for justice and truth; it is their capacity to mobilize not only relatives and friends but also activists working for other causes, and even people who are not particularly politically active but are becoming aware of this reality of police violence and racism; and, finally, it is their determination not to forget, not to accept the official versions of the facts, not to settle for predictable court decisions.

Thus, a network emerged, formed of several collectives fighting for recognition and compensation for stolen lives, as the name of one of the groups put it. While the divisions and conflicts, sometimes arising out of personal rivalries presented under the guise of ideological differences, should not be understated, it is still remarkable that such nation-wide solidarity was created. In any case, because it was a local movement, the Justice for Angelo Collective managed to remain separate from these tensions. Representatives of other campaigns participated in the many events it organized: the fundraising concerts, the public debate on prison, the film showing of a documentary made by another collective, and the commemorative events held two months, six months, one year and two years after Angelo's death. In return, the collective joined demonstrations for Lamine Dieng, Wissam El-Yamni, Adama Traoré and others, as well as the Rosa Parks Collective, which campaigns against state racism. Angelo's sister often spoke at these events. Her remarks were all the more powerful because it is rare for Travellers to speak out in campaigns against police violence and racism. Words of minorities, we are the majority!, declares a flyer published by the Justice for Angelo Collective. The young woman and her comrades in struggle thus draw an unlikely link between people from the projects and travelling people. Unlikely because, in the past, relations between the two have often been tense.

Locally, there was even an attempt to develop a public education program in a poor neighborhood of the nearby city. The idea was that young men from minorities, whether they are black, Arab or Travellers, as they said, share similar experiences of stigmatization and marginalization, of police brutality and stop-and-search, of court appearances and prison sentences – experiences that are reproduced from generation to generation and thus eventually become routine, including for those subjected to them. The aim was therefore to break this tendency to normalize practices of exception toward them. However, the project never came to fruition, as the long-drawn-out negotiations with the municipal authorities failed to reach a successful conclusion. But the urge to create a bridge between struggles, to move the Travellers' cause beyond its potential isolation within the Roma culture championed by some community organizations, and to understand solidarity in cross-community terms through the issues of discrimination and racism was a guiding spirit of the Justice for Angelo Collective from its inception.

It was more difficult to establish this kind of relationship between campaigns for victims of police violence belonging to minorities and campaigns for those who had suffered such violence during street demonstrations. This compartmentalization of struggles is not new. There are at least two reasons for it. First, the conditions in which this violence occurs are different and arise out of different forms of law enforcement. Police violence against minorities derives from everyday tensions that are exacerbated at the moment of some arrests; it relates to what is often termed public security. Police violence against demonstrators arises during one-off events; it originates in practices described as public order. Second, the groups targeted by these strategies, and hence the victims of this violence, belong to different social worlds and live in different places. The experience of young working-class men of immigrant origin living in housing projects has little in common with that of middle-class people participating in political gatherings in the city center. The two rarely meet, still less in campaign activities.

However, the recent toughening of government policy on crime prevention and the growing awareness of police brutality that has emerged as a result have led to the beginnings of a rapprochement between the two groups. The Yellow Vest movement marked a turning point, with hundreds of serious injuries caused by Flash-Ball rounds and Sting-Ball grenades. On the twelfth Saturday of Yellow Vest demonstration, the slogan was: End police violence! From the housing projects to the Yellow Vests! Three months later, the march called to mark two years since the GIGN's fatal intervention was attended both by people from the Yellow Vest movement, some of whom had come from a neighboring town, and by Travellers, under the Romani flag with its sixteen-spoked wheel. But in contrast to what had happened in the larger cities of the region, where there had been clashes between demonstrators and police, once again, here, confrontation was avoided.

At one of these public events, Angelo's sister, turning to the members of other collectives who had come together in memory of one of their own, said: Equality does not exist for us. All we have left is fraternity. She added: When we march for one, we march for all! Her words hit home. They endured.

XI

Mourning

How could they mourn? While Angelo's sister sometimes says that the fight is her therapy, it does not heal the pain of the loss of her brother. His death is an open wound – a wound that will remain open, as far as the family is concerned, until the truth is told and justice is done. Not a day goes by without the parents and their children referring to what happened that afternoon, without their cursing those they call the killers, without their despairing at the decision taken by the examining magistrate not to refer the case to court. Since the tragedy, their lives have been turned upside down. They cannot pull themselves away from the sequence of violence and humiliation that ended in the death of their son and brother. They viewed the announcement by the first magistrate, that the two officers who fired the shots had been placed under investigation, as an encouraging sign. The ruling of the second magistrate dismissing the case was a knockout blow. A glimmer of hope remained with the appeal procedure. It was snuffed out when the initial decision was upheld. Not that they had really had any confidence in the justice system. But, all the same, as they saw it the circumstances of the death were so obviously outrageous, abnormal, unjustifiable that it seemed to them that any impartial judge would be able to see it. When the final appeal failed, they felt betrayed. They had not even been allowed to attend the hearing at the appeals court, which had been held behind closed doors. Probably for fear of the family's reactions. As if they had not sufficiently demonstrated, at the various events they had organized, their ability to contain their emotions.

On the day after the tragedy, Angelo's sister went to the courthouse to ask for psychological support from the victim assistance service. Not for herself, she said. For her parents, who lived through the death of their son without being able to do anything to prevent it and were floored by grief. Also for her little boy, who was present during the operation and whose reaction to such a devastating event was hard to imagine. We can't do anything for you, said the person to whom she spoke. But come on, she insisted, when there's a terrorist attack, a bus accident, a suicide in a school, there's always a psychological team providing support to people affected. In the GIGN operation, her parents were witnesses to what amounted to a war scene. And their child was killed. The woman was sorry. She called someone, who said that the best thing would be to consult the family doctor. Hearing this response, Angelo's sister understood that a distinction is drawn between the families of victims seen as innocent and the relatives of victims seen as guilty. The former are imagined to have suffered trauma meriting the help of mental health specialists. The latter are not. The former have a right to compassion. The latter are treated with indifference.

Once they had returned home, Angelo's family had to organize a funeral. The body had been taken to the forensic pathology institute forty miles away. When they were told the body had been released, they thought it would be brought to them. They were put straight. It was up to them to organize the return and pay the costs. In the travelling community, it is customary for the deceased's extended family to sit in vigil over the body for several days in its last home. But in view of the exceptional circumstances

of the death, they decided to take the body to the funeral
parlor in the neighboring city. The parents found it hard to
imagine it in their house, riddled with bullets, sliced open
and stitched back up again after the autopsy, a macabre
and painful presence reminding them of the tragic circumstances in which he died.

The wake lasted five nights. Five sleepless nights. The
neighbor, a retired winegrower, kindly lent his field next
door for the many visitors to camp. Each evening eighty
people, sometimes even more, gathered around fires with
coffee to honor the deceased and speak of their memories
of him. But his parents, brother, sisters and children, still
in shock from his violent death, were unable to participate in these conversations. Stunned by the tragedy and
harrowed by the conditions in which it occurred, they
could not find the serenity normally befitting such wakes,
and they sought to return to the closeness of their small
family circle to talk among themselves of what had just
happened. Coming together with the collective was more
than they could manage. During the day, they were taken
up by the many practical tasks involved in settling administrative issues, organizing the funeral, meeting the lawyer,
filing a complaint. The burial was held on the sixth day,
a few miles from their home, in the cemetery where all
the members of the family are laid to rest. The coffin was
placed in the vault alongside that of Angelo's grandfather.

It was months before the family could begin to remember happy times spent with Angelo rather than passing the
days going over and over his final moments, expressing
their resentment at law enforcement and the justice system.
It was more than two years before they felt strong enough
to grill food again, because the thought of the barbecue
and the smell of meat plunged them, despite themselves,
right back into the nightmare of the GIGN operation. Often
the father wakes in the night and cannot get back to sleep.
Then he goes to the window, lights a cigarette, thinks of
his son, and replays the events. Three or four times a week,
the sister drives to the cemetery and waters the plants on

her brother's grave. When she goes a few days without making this pilgrimage, she misses it badly.

Thus, paradoxically, Angelo is more present to his family dead than when he was alive. When he was in prison, and even when he was out, they often did not see him or hear from him for months. They did not miss him. They knew that was his way of being in the world. Unsettled and precarious. But his death, and the circumstances in which it occurred, tore a gaping hole in their lives that the attitude of the authorities, and the magistrates' decisions, only widened. The thought of this tragedy, which society had been unable to resolve in a way they would have found acceptable, is with them day and night.

The pain is not only the absence of Angelo, the loss of a son and a brother. Not even only what his family see as the injustice of justice. In the circumstances of his death itself, there was an indignity that probably neither the gendarmes nor the judges can understand, so much is it already, more or less consciously, part of how they see travelling people. It can be grasped simply by hearing how often the family speak of their community, noting how they were treated in their own home, seeing how their words were marginalized or distorted during the investigation. It was the indignity of dying hunted down like a rat, the family members repeat to one another. Trapped in a corner, dragged through the dust, sullied in that final moment. One point constantly returns in their conversations. Angelo was wearing sneakers without socks when he died. Their voices break and tears come to their eyes when they speak of this. But who will understand that indignity could reside in such a minuscule detail, a detail that, for his family, nevertheless represents an irreparable defilement?

In a corner of the garden at the family home a white sedan is parked. It is Angelo's last car. The one in which he drove to his parents' home for the lunch he never had. The one in which he travelled from place to place in the region, like the wandering nomad he had always been since his teenage years and had become even more in the circumstances of what the newspapers were calling his escape. The car in which he slept with his son in the surrounding countryside, less to hide from the gendarmes, who could easily have found him when he went to visit his former girlfriend or his eldest daughter, than to avoid creating problems for anyone who invited him for the night and might be charged with harboring a fugitive if he was caught. The car in which, had the gendarmes come a few minutes earlier, he might have been arrested, as his son had been, without violence. If things had gone this way, he would still be alive.

For three years, the car has stayed in the same place. It was parked on the property shortly after the tragedy and it has not moved since. Nobody touches it. The children are not allowed to play in it. Nothing has been altered inside. There is still his sleeping bag, a pillow on his seat, a pair of socks, an empty soda bottle – humble traces of an itinerant, fragile life, the life of a Traveller who, unlike the rest of his family, had never really managed to settle down. Or, rather, had never wanted to. The father keeps saying, without conviction, that someday they must get rid of this bulky yet precious relic, but his daughter insists it be left as it was on that fateful day when the gendarmes took her brother from her. Sometimes, she confides sadly, she sits in what was his seat, at the steering wheel, to be with him in thought.

XII

Biography

There are two very distinct versions of Angelo's biography. There is the one reconstituted by the justice system and reproduced by the media. It is nothing more than a criminal record comprising twenty-one offenses, most of them minor. The prison sentences are unusually long relative to the seriousness of the crimes, mainly owing to the fact that they are repeat offenses and that, over time, suspended sentences and probation orders have been activated. A few exploits stand out from this list, however, and these are highlighted by the gendarmes and the magistrates: by the gendarmes to justify the massive resources deployed to arrest him and by the magistrates to establish a profile that fits with the account on which the argument for dismissing the case is based. These include a conviction for attempting to ram into a gendarmerie vehicle at a roadside check, one for robbery with violence aggravated by an attempt to run a person down, and one for throwing stolen items at the police to enable him to escape. There was also the matter of a fight in which two other Travellers were injured, which occurred only a few weeks before the GIGN operation but was not brought to court. Finally, there is the presentation of him as a man on the run after he failed to return to prison. The picture is certainly dark. But there is another, brighter, biography, recounted by his family. Not an idealized one, and his father comments bluntly: He screwed up so many times! But it is more than just a catalogue of violations of the law. We might simply call this other biography his life.

Following the death of his mother in a car accident when he was eighteen months old, he was raised by an aunt. When he was nine, he returned to his father, who had remarried in the meantime and had just had a little girl. He immediately felt at home in his new family. The person that legal documents identify as his stepmother, he straightaway called mom, and he saw the three children of the second marriage as his sisters and brother. His father is from a Traveller family and, when he was younger, would indeed travel the region with his first wife, whom he calls a *manouche*, in a horse-drawn caravan. He is so nostalgic for this time that, when it rains, he goes out under the tin roof over the terrace to hear the rain falling like he used to. His second wife describes herself as a country woman, who comes from the village where they then settled, but for her family she is a *gadji*, a woman who does not belong to the travelling community. The couple stayed for a while on the land that belonged to the paternal grandparents.

Angelo did not shine at school, and it seems that he did not finish the special general and vocational education program in which students with learning disabilities are placed. And then at home he had to help his father, who was a scrap metal merchant, and he made a little pocket money for himself by picking up metal at the dump for recycling. He preferred nature to school and would spend long hours fishing in the nearby river, sometimes with friends. At night, when the sky was clear, he taught the older of his two sisters to recognize the stars and the constellations. He was crazy about scooters, on which he used to take her out for a spin. He was keen on auto mechanics, in fact, though an apprenticeship at a training center would certainly not have been to his taste. He was not stable enough.

He had his first interaction with the justice system at the age of fourteen. He had taken an apple from a branch overhanging the wall of a garden in the village. The owner had seen him and filed a complaint. His mother had to go with him to the juvenile court, where the judge lectured both of them, telling them to their great surprise that, even if it was within reach above the sidewalk, the fruit was still on the tree and was therefore the property of the person residing on the land where the tree was planted. The act of picking the apple was therefore a theft. But the justification they were given convinced them of only one thing: it was because they were Travellers that they were reported to the police and summoned to court for such a trifling act.

He was eighteen when he left the family home. At the time, his father was in prison. His young girlfriend was pregnant. They had their first daughter, then their son two years later. In order to support the family, he recovered pallets thrown out by shops and sold them on. At twenty-two, he went to prison for the first time. He was driving without a valid license and without insurance. At a roadside check the gendarmes, who had probably recognized him, signaled him to stop. He did not comply. He accelerated. The charge was changed to failing to stop with an attempt to ram into a gendarmerie vehicle. His family were present when he appeared in court. In the hearing, the public defender, perhaps in an attempt to elicit the judges' sympathy, presented him as just a little chicken thief, which is the habitual pejorative way of designating Travellers. At the time the remark amused the family, though he had never been caught stealing any winged creature or anything else. But, if it was meant to soften the hearts of the judges, the joke fell short. It did not prevent an unconditional prison sentence with committal order.

It is difficult to say to what extent the criminal career on which he embarked when he got out of jail a year and half later was linked to relationships he had developed in prison. He stole, he got caught, he was sent back to jail.

He was therefore not present at the birth of his second son and only met him once he got out. Once again, his stay on the outside was brief. During his third prison sentence, his partner told him she was leaving him, and shortly afterward she abandoned their three children, who were taken in by the older of his two sisters. When he got out, his parents put him up and he was able to look after his children again. But, with no job, no vehicle, no driving license, no personal resources, no welfare benefits, his situation was extremely precarious. He stole a car and was arrested as he was stealing copper in industrial premises. Back to jail.

A more stable period follows his release two years later. He has a new girlfriend who is not a Traveller. She is the mother of a little girl. She gives him strong encouragement to change his way of life. He takes a course in vine-pruning at a viticulture school. Both work in vineyards in the region. Depending on the season, they are taken on for pruning, debudding and harvesting. Certificates from his employers testify to his qualities as a committed, reliable worker with a sense of initiative. In the months when he is without work, he signs on at the job center, receives his unemployment benefit and looks for a new contract. He is interested in what goes on in the world, in environmental issues, in politics. A brief happy interval in his adult life. The last photos his family have of him show a cheerful young man, working among the vines, driving a tractor, taking his children pony riding, teaching his girlfriend's daughter to swim or ride a bike.

But financial difficulties very soon catch up with him. Court costs, old fines, financial compensation to civil parties, the child support deducted at source from his income. His meager wages go on repaying his accumulated debts. The sums due seem enormous. He says his life is shot. He has the feeling he is being pushed down just when he was beginning to pull himself up. And he plunges in again. Takes part in robberies. Is caught. Returns to jail on remand. The prison is nearly one hundred and twenty miles from his parents' home. He puts in a request for a transfer to be closer to his family, but it takes a long time to be processed. He knows nobody in the prison. He feels isolated.

The lawyer who got to know him well during the months when various cases were being examined by the magistrate, who grouped them together so as to issue a single verdict and hence a single sentence, senses during their meetings that he is suffering, that he needs support. She describes him as a calm, gentle man with whom contact is easy and direct. When the judge questions him about a petty theft, he replies without equivocation. If he is the perpetrator, he admits it. If he denies he was involved, he is to be believed. He does not lie. Nor does he give up his accomplices. Although it is known that several of his crimes were committed on the order of others, he never provides any names and consequently appears in court alone. He is considered as truthful in front of the judge as he is loyal to his associates.

The trial is held. He is sentenced to twenty-seven months' imprisonment, with the time spent on remand to be taken into account. Normally, once the verdict has been pronounced and the individual is returned to custody for a moment before his transfer to prison, the guards allow the family to speak with him for a few minutes to comfort him. This time they are not permitted to do so. With a lump in their throats, they see him handcuffed and taken away under close guard. A year later, he gets his first home leave. The following day he does not return. He is then deemed a fugitive and a wanted notice is put out for him. He leads a precarious existence, inviting himself to spend a few nights with friends or relatives, then moving on to others. After two months he meets up with his girlfriend again and moves in with her. But he feels hunted. Eventually he returns to his itinerant life. On the morning of his death, on some level refusing to recognize his situation as a fugitive, he speaks with his elder daughter about his wish to sign on at the job center and look for work. As if it were still possible for him to have a normal life.

All those who knew Angelo – his family of course, but
also the professionals in the justice system who had dealings with him – agree that he was not dangerous. His
criminal past consisted mainly of driving without a license,
after he lost it and did not have the money to retake
his test, and thefts with the aggravating circumstances of
repeat offenses, escalation, breaking and entering, and
sometimes having been committed in a residence. He had
never used a weapon to resist arrest, not even the pocket
knife he always kept on him. He sometimes fought with
other Travellers, including a few months before his death
when he was attacked by members of another family and
wounded two of his adversaries, but he had never been
known to assault anyone outside of his community. The
picture is far from that painted by the gendarmes to justify
their operation and make the scene in the lean-to plausible.

Behind the disturbing portrait painted by the authorities,
there was what the Justice for Angelo Collective called the
prison spiral in which the young Traveller found himself
caught. Between the ages of twenty-two and thirty-seven,
he spent most of his time in prison. It is undeniable that
he had committed a number of offenses that the judges
could not fail to take into account when they had to pass
sentence. But what was their aim when they sentenced
him to prison terms that the aggravating circumstances
– easy to find in his case – allowed them to extend, and
to the payment of compensation and interest to civil parties, blocking any possibility of stabilizing his financial
situation? Each time he came out he felt paralyzed by an
ever darker reality, finding himself without money, without
work, without transportation, without any prospect of
coming back to normal life, with nothing to his name but
an increasingly long criminal record. Under these conditions, falling back into crime was almost inevitable, even
once he had succeeded in embarking on a new life. A story
like Angelo's, admitted the lawyer who was the last to
defend him in court, has to raise the question of the limits
of justice. Not only did the punishments handed down

have no deterrent effect, but they actually led to what they were supposed to prevent.

It had all started with driving without a license, aggravated by a refusal to comply with a roadside vehicle check, which judicial language had translated into the disturbing formulation of attempting to ram into a gendarmerie vehicle. It was the beginning of a vicious cycle from which Angelo had never managed to break out. Now that she thinks about that first appearance in court, his sister remembers their lawyer's words with shame and anger. Chicken thief. There is no such thing as minor humiliation, minor stigmatization. She understands how much the phrase crystallizes the common prejudice against Travellers. Thieves by definition, even when they haven't stolen anything. That is where everything starts. That, she says to herself, is what has led to us being here today.

XIII

Investigation

It was the work of two judges. The first conducted the judicial examination; the second took the final decision. The first issued letters rogatory, questioned the officers and placed them under investigation, deposed the witnesses, including the members of the family, and visited the scene of the events to check how any warnings could be heard there; the second studied the case file and drew up the ruling dismissing the case. This unusual but not unique situation is due simply to the transfer of the examining magistrate, at her request, and her replacement. In general, any cases pending are the subject of communication from one to the other; this may be accompanied by an opinion from the departing judge, which the incoming one is obviously at liberty to follow or not. In this case, there was indeed a communication and an opinion on the case, as the judges privately admitted, but the rules of judicial confidentiality obviously mean that there is no way of knowing either what the first magistrate suggested or whether her colleague followed her recommendation.

It is the public prosecutor who decides whether a judicial investigation should be opened. In this case it was almost unavoidable, given that, according to the terms of the introductory indictment, there was serious and consistent evidence of the perpetration of violence with use or threat of a weapon leading to involuntary homicide. There are two examining magistrates in the criminal court, and it was the one who was on duty that week whom the public prosecutor asked to take on the judicial investigation. In view of the gravity and complexity of the case, the judge nevertheless, as a precaution, requested a joint referral with her colleague. But in reality she ended up conducting the whole of the procedure.

When she took the case on, however, a lot of evidence had already been amassed from the immediate investigation at the scene: photographs and detailed descriptions of the locations and material evidence; records of statements made by the officers placed under investigation and witnesses just after the events; a report from the re-enactment at the location of the tragedy; samples of material and balaclavas, gloves, bulletproof vests, machine pistols, tasers and knives taken into evidence for various examinations, including DNA testing; blood tests for drugs and alcohol; autopsy and ballistics reports; and a summary drawn up by the criminal investigation officers.

Having been assigned the case seven days after the tragedy, as is normal legal procedure, the judge thus arrives relatively late to the events, when major elements of the investigation have been put together, already pointing the resolution of the case in a certain direction. All the statements from the immediate aftermath – in other words, before the men under investigation and the witnesses had had time to prepare together for the questions they were asked – have been taken. Moreover, owing to the circumstances, the GIGN men were questioned by their very colleagues from the General Inspectorate of the Gendarmerie. Besides, the reconstruction was staged without the presence of witnesses from the victim's family, with the autopsy and ballistics data sent to the investigators beforehand, allowing them to take these into account when the GIGN men re-enacted the scene. Furthermore, the public prosecutor has already communicated his provi-

sional conclusions to the press, validating the gendarmes'
version subject to any new evidence from the investigation. Finally, the summary report from the immediate
aftermath investigation by the General Inspectorate of the
Gendarmerie has indicated that there is no contradiction
between the GIGN men's statements and the results from
examination of evidence. In other words, when the examining magistrate takes on the case, the ground has already
been well signposted by law-enforcement institutions and
the public prosecutor.

Nevertheless, she has theoretically broad prerogatives
with regard to anything that may contribute to revealing
the truth, including issuing letters rogatory and summons
to suspects and witnesses. In addition, she insists that she
remains independent of the public prosecutor's office and
that the public prosecutor does not interfere in the conduct
of the judicial investigation. In proof of this, following her
initial questioning of the two who fired the fatal shots,
she decides to place them under formal investigation. This
move, which suggests that she does not take for granted
the theory of legitimate self-defense, does not of course
call into question the presumption of innocence of the two
men. But both the family and the gendarmes, obviously
with contrasting reactions, interpret it as a recognition
that the version hitherto presented by the GIGN and the
public prosecutor is problematic. However, the decision is
not accompanied by security restrictions that would further deepen the impression of suspicion. The two officers
remain at liberty and even retain use of their weapons.

This decision, quite remarkable in its deviation from the
line of interpretation put forward until then, is reinforced
by two letters rogatory that appear to point in the same
direction. The first requires the deposition, at the request
of the civil parties to the case, of the emergency response
doctor who indicated, in a recorded exchange with his
colleague in dispatch, that, to use his terms, the guy was
not armed and that he himself was required to exhibit
complete discretion. It is easy to grasp the importance

of these words, which contradict the gendarmes' version and moreover suggest an attempt to influence a witness. Indeed, the doctor's discomfort and his muddled denials add to the confusion of his statements. The second letter is a request for transportation to the site, a far from simple operation since, in addition to two examining magistrates, a representative of the public prosecutor's office, two stenographers, three investigation officers, an official of the General Inspectorate of the Gendarmerie, and the family of the victim, it requires the attendance of a gendarmerie unit in case of public disorder, as the requisition puts it. The exercise, which is conducted in the rain, enables the judge to see the location where the events took place and, in particular, to check how sound travels between the lumber room and the locations of the witnesses at the time of the killing. It reveals that a warning given inside the shed can be heard distinctly from where the father, the mother and the sister-in-law were held, and a little less clearly from the place where the brother and uncle were grounded. Therefore, either the family are lying when they say they heard nothing in the few seconds following the gendarmes' entry into the lean-to, or the gendarmes are trying to mislead the courts by stating that they announced their presence, that the victim shouted, and that warnings were given.

When she was assigned the case, the examining magistrate understood straightaway that it was doubly sensitive. On the one hand, she knew that, above and beyond the family of the deceased, the whole community of travelling people already nursed a mistrust of the justice system and, more broadly, of state institutions, a mistrust that several recent experiences in the region had only helped to foster. On the other, she understood that the involvement of gendarmes and, what was more, their elite unit gave the events a particular slant that could generate a strong media reaction, even though at this point the local press seemed to have put a lid on it by accepting the official version without comment. Thus, while the pressure she felt as she investigated the case was not due to direct interventions from the public prosecutor's department or other bodies, it was bound up with issues that could not fail to crystallize her decision. A decision, moreover, that was asymmetrical in its significance and its implications, since a ruling of dismissal would indicate that the men placed under examination were innocent, while a referral to the high criminal court would merely lead to their being charged but not in any way imply their guilt, which could have been established only at the end of the trial. However, the examining magistrate's departure for another jurisdiction released her from having to come down on either side.

During her statement before her, the victim's sister declared that, in her view, her brother's death was an execution, pure and simple. The judge replied, probably in an effort to calm her, that it could have been an accident. No interpretation is offered here of these words, for they are not without ambiguity. The expression could mean that the officers, facing an attack, fired clumsily without intending to kill or that, panicking, they fired even though they were not threatened in any way by a weapon. In either case, it would make it impossible to substantiate legitimate self-defense. While the true meaning of these words remains buried in judicial confidentiality, the formulation nevertheless suggests that a different ruling was possible.

XIV
Dismissal

The ruling was therefore made by the examining magistrate who had just taken up office and to whom the case had been passed by her predecessor. Her job was to dispose of the case, as legal parlance has it. Unquestionably, it is difficult, in such situation, to get a precise idea just by reading the statements and expert witness reports. To be sure, one brings a fresh eye to the scrutiny of the facts, perhaps more detached from the emotions and the pressures that may have arisen at one point or another. But this advantage cannot replace detailed knowledge of the case, the gradual uncovering of evidence, direct interaction with the witnesses and the men under investigation, the conviction that gradually forms and the doubts that persist. There are questions one would have liked to ask or additional information one would have sought. Not that it is impossible to do this, but, in a case such as this, the magistrate understands that she must not take too long to make a decision. The public prosecutor has asked her to treat it as a priority. It is a sensitive case. People are awaiting a decision. Both the travelling community, whose reactions if the case is dismissed are still a source of anxiety, and the gendarmes, whose protests if the case is referred to trial can easily be imagined. While in theory the public prosecutor does not intervene at this stage to guide the examining magistrate's decision, he has clearly indicated from the start that he accepted the version of events presented by the officers and has then kept firmly to this position, expressed once again in his statements to court.

Are the charges against the two men who fired the shots sufficient to send them to trial? Is there serious and consistent evidence of a manifest error in the use of their weapons that led to the death of the individual they were to arrest? These are the questions the judge must answer. She bases her response on the data from the immediate aftermath investigation, which had already come down on the side of legitimate self-defense, and on information from the judicial investigation, which supplemented the preliminary with new statements and several expert witness reports. She also has the public prosecutor's recommendation on the case and the observations of the lawyers for the officers and for the family. A year and a half after the events, she is thus able to draw up the twenty-one pages of her ruling dismissing the case. It is one of her first decisions, not only in her new jurisdiction but also as an examining magistrate, as up to now she has adjudicated only civil court cases.

Since this document temporarily closes the case and is largely repeated in the examining chamber at the court of appeals, it is worth examining it in detail. A judicial document giving the argument for a decision is always an exercise in rhetoric. But, rather than persuading the reader, its aim is to justify a judgment on a case from a legal point of view.

It sometimes happens that, in an official document, there is a single detail that gives the key to its reading, in some cases even unbeknown to its authors. There is such a detail in the ruling dismissing the case. In order to establish the absence of intention to cause death, the ruling states that the autopsy located the bullet wounds in a region between the thorax and the top of the pelvis, but that none had penetrated a vital organ such as the head or the heart, and therefore concludes that the officers used their weapons purely to contain their target, who was not allowing them to apprehend him. This point is essential to the dismissal of the case, for it means that it can be asserted that homicidal intent is manifestly excluded, prompting the judge to conclude that the offense of voluntary violence leading to involuntary homicide is clearly established.

But what does the autopsy report say? There are five entry wounds, four of them in the thorax. Examination of the thoracic cavity shows that one of the bullets passed through the pericardium, the right atrium and the right ventricle. Thus, the heart definitely was penetrated. Pierced through. There is a hemothorax, with a liter of blood on the right side and more than a liter on the left, caused by the wound in the heart, as well as multiple lacerations to both lungs caused by bullet trajectories. Adding in the three hundred milliliters of hemoperitoneum in the abdomen caused by lesions to the liver and right kidney, half of the victim's blood volume flowed out within a few seconds. In sum, not only was the heart indeed penetrated, as were the lungs, but the massive hemorrhage that resulted caused almost instantaneous death owing to the rupture of the cardiac cycle. Given that the report from the forensic pathology institute is clear in this respect, it is significant that the ruling dismissing the case contradicts it so blatantly, repeating the public prosecutor's statements word for word and ignoring the remarks of the family's counsel. Moreover, even if none of the bullets had penetrated the heart, the fact that four of them entered the thorax weakens the argument that the shots were intended purely to control the target, as the officers claim, as this would have implied aiming at the lower limbs. Why, then, feature this point, so easily invalidated, in the ruling dismissing the case?

It could of course be supposed that this is simply a trace inadvertently left in the text owing to inattentive reading of the autopsy report and placing too much trust in the recommendations of the public prosecutor. This might be the case if it appeared outside of any context. But it occurs against a general strategy of excluding facts that might contradict the gendarmes' version. To take just the autopsy, which is supplemented by the ballistics analysis, there is a crucial piece of information that is not taken into consideration. It relates to the bullet paths. The five bullets that hit the victim were all fired with a top-down trajectory, four of them into the upper part of the thorax, entering the body at very marked angles to the horizontal, one even almost vertical. The two men who fired the fatal shots could therefore only have been well above the victim, and very close to him. The five gendarmes who were in the lean-to state that their target was standing; the two who fired describe themselves as facing him, therefore at the same height, one of them also having fired after he had fallen, and therefore well below the victim. The judge's ruling does include the autopsy in the list of investigations conducted and cites its principal results. But it slightly modifies the conclusion of the ballistics report, by substituting one adverb for another and placing it in inverted commas as if it were a quotation, so that the bullet paths are described as probably, rather than generally, from the front to the back and from above to below. Moreover, it does not introduce the autopsy report into the discussion arguing for the dismissal, preferring rather to emphasize once more that the shots were not localized in the vital organs. Through the alteration of the technical expert's conclusion and its disappearance from the final argument, essential objective evidence is thus omitted from the discussion.

And this is especially significant because the only bullet path data that is discussed relates to the reconstruction conducted the day after the events. The ruling notes a bullet hole in the ceiling of the store, backing up the story of the second officer's fall, and asserts that the reconstruction of the shots thus correlates with the autopsy observations, without mentioning the discrepancy between the assertions of the officers, who say they were facing their target

when they fired, and the entry angles of the bullets, which
suggest they were above the victim. One further piece
of information from the autopsy could also have been
mentioned, though it constitutes only ancillary evidence.
Two of the five gendarmes affirm that at the beginning of
the interaction, before the man pulled out his knife, they
tried to take him unarmed and that he managed to slip
their grasp. One might therefore expect to see anatomical
signs on the victim's upper limbs. But autopsy incisions
of the upper arm and forearm found no subcutaneous
blood leakage indicative of a struggle. By contrast, the two
parents, whom the GIGN men also seized by the arms, both
exhibited hematomas at the time of their arrest.

In short, just as an object inadvertently left at the scene
of a crime can serve as evidence that will help to identify
the perpetrator, here the note of the absence of injury to
a vital organ, carelessly left in the ruling, is revealed as
the signature of a strategy of argument. This assertion,
being easy to disprove, actually invites the reader to look
for other signs. There are plenty of them, in addition to
those already mentioned. The repeated testimony of the
five members of the family present during the operation,
that the sound of the shots came almost immediately after
the gendarmes entered the lean-to, without any warning
or other words being heard, is replaced in the final discussion by the statement that some of them supposedly
heard shouts but could not hear exact words. From this it
is deduced that the gendarmes did signal their presence. In
fact, it was only the sister-in-law, in her first statement just
after the event, who said she thought she heard a shout,
but she later took this back. The variations and indeed
contradictions between the versions of the five GIGN men,
for example on whether their target was yelling abuse
or made no sound, whether he raised his hands in the
air or took a boxing stance, whether four of them fell or
only one, whether there was a scuffle on the floor or the
victim collapsed unconscious, are not taken up. The first
officer's declaration that while facing the man he never

saw his knife, which led one of the criminal investigation officers to ask him how he could shoot someone who was unarmed, is not raised as a point that might introduce doubt, or is at least worthy of discussion. The recorded remarks of the doctor called to the scene, that the victim was unarmed and that the gendarmes asked him to keep silent, are disregarded on the grounds simply that this was an unfamiliar context for him. Even the fact that the officers admit they gave no warning before firing is elided, as the ruling conversely states that they gave several in accordance with the regular protocol.

Alongside this, the portrait drawn of Angelo corroborates the gendarmes' description of his attitude. The recap of his criminal history, including six convictions involving violence that are appended to the case file, even mentions that during one recent brawl he threatened to return with a Kalashnikov, taking seriously a threat that was highly unrealistic in view of the weaponry of Travellers. The way the features of his personality and biography provided by his family are selected is also indicative of the orientation given to how the victim is presented. During their initial depositions, taken just a few hours after the events, his relatives were astonished when they were questioned less about the traumatic events they had just experienced than about the deceased, his character, his concerns, his plans, his way of life, his drug habits – to the extent that his father, shocked at the turn the questioning was taking, decided to put an end to it. Quoting extracts from the statements of his relatives, the ruling depicts his son as a cheerful, generous, kind man who liked to laugh and was not violent, but whom it was dangerous to annoy, who had a bad experience of prison and in any case had no intention of returning there, who was undermined by debts for compensation for civil parties and who used heroin, who was quick to pull out his knife and had seriously wounded a member of a rival family. The profile is thus drawn of a man determined not to be arrested and ready to use a weapon. The reference to addiction is repeated several times and, despite the fact that the toxicology analysis recorded only marijuana and an opiate substitute medication in the blood, the reported reaction to the taser shots, which is presented as a state of furious rage or even a fit, is explained in terms of intake of drugs, specifically cocaine. Traces of cocaine were certainly found but, as the toxicology report states, their presence only in the bile indicates that some time had elapsed since it was taken, that the stimulating effects had worn off, and that the killing possibly even occurred in the secondary depressive phase.

All of this taken together, it is clear that it would be wrong to imagine that the rhetorical structure of the ruling dismissing the case is based on a weighing of inculpatory and exculpatory evidence. The case is not discussed in terms of which aspects tend to exonerate and, conversely, which to incriminate the officers. There is no critical analysis of the unlikely scenarios, the discrepancies between statements and the conflicts with the evidence, either to the detriment or in favor of the men who fired. The for and against are not balanced, as the symbolic scales of justice suggest they should be. The argument is developed as a straightforward demonstration that retains the evidence supporting what is being demonstrated while modifying or discarding that which goes against it. The conclusion is therefore not the end point of the reasoning: it is the starting point. This is not to suggest that the magistrate did not commit to examining the facts in all conscience, as she put it. But what is certain is that all the arguments adduced in her ruling tend in the same direction. At the cost of twisting some facts and ignoring others. At the cost of following the public prosecutor's statements to the extent of repeating some passages word for word.

Thus, it became clear that legitimate self-defense could be established and that Article L.435-I of the Public Security Code had been respected. The man was threatening the life or bodily integrity of several gendarmes. They first attempted to persuade him to drop his knife. They then tried in vain to subdue him unarmed. After this, they tried taser shots, without result. As a last resort, they had no other solution than to use their firearms. Even then the officers had avoided hitting a vital organ.

One final piece of evidence was cited to add credibility to this account of the events. The ruling recalled that the public prosecutor had initiated legal proceedings against Angelo for violence toward officers invested with public authority, which the GIGN accused him of on the day of his arrest. These proceedings were of course closed, since the prosecution was cancelled following his death. But, presented as guilty, it was difficult for him to aspire to the status of victim. Only his death spared him further incrimination.

No doubt it would have been hard for the judge to come to a different decision and hence to write the dismissal ruling differently. Given that she had only recently taken up office as examining magistrate and that, moreover, she was just starting out in the role, that she came in at a late stage in the judicial investigation, and that the tensions around the case were palpable, she had to rule on it in the awareness that she did not have all the facts and knowing that all the weight of her institution rested on her shoulders. But, under these conditions, what truth did her decision articulate?

XV
Truth

For that matter, how can the truth ever be known? In the case of the death of Angelo, it seems diffracted into several versions. There is the truth of the gendarmes and that of the family. And, even within the former, there are variations. Consider one specific element: what was heard between the moment the officers entered and the moment they fired, in that brief interval that ended in tragedy. This is a key point, since it determines, first, whether there was a confrontation in the lean-to and, second, whether warnings or orders were given before the shots were fired.

The gendarmes' and the parents' versions cannot be reconciled with one another. The five men who were inside the small lumber room describe the uproar of a confrontation in which Angelo's yelling, apparently incomprehensible since none of them is able to state precisely what he was saying, mingled with their own shouts, first calling: Police, police, come out of there!, then shouting: Knife, knife!, then repeatedly ordering: Drop your weapon!, and finally calling out: I'm hit! On top of these various shouts there is the noise of crates tipping over and bodies falling. One senior officer who was in the courtyard even says he heard his colleagues, when they entered, shout: Target contact – a remarkable utterance, which he is, however, the only one to mention. The father, the uncle, the brother, the mother and the sister-in-law, the first three lying on the ground, the other two sitting on the steps of the caravan, all five only a few yards from the wide open door, on the contrary describe a very short silence, broken only by the boots of the gendarmes stumbling over objects in the interior, before the sudden burst of gunfire, followed by a low groan. No shouts, no orders, they state categorically. So which truth is to be retained? And indeed – more fundamentally – what is truth?

In general, a statement is considered to be true if it articulates an actual fact. In this case philosophers speak of correspondence, for what is said corresponds to what happened. Angelo had a knife in his hand, or he did not. The gendarmes instructed him to give himself up, or they did not. In each case, one of the assertions is necessarily true and the other necessarily false. But how is one to know which is which? In effect, this truth of the facts is neither directly accessible to the magistrates and the investigators nor more broadly to those attempting to discover it. They base their conclusions on the statements made to them by the protagonists, which may differ, as is the case here. The five gendarmes recount, with significant variations, their version of a scene in which they are active participants. The five members of the victim's family present an entirely different version of this same scene, of which they are the auditory witnesses.

So how to choose between the two? Magistrates and investigators seek additional evidence that would corroborate one version or the other. This may be objective, such as the discovery of a weapon close to the body that supports the account of an attack, or subjective, through the gathering of other testimonies that contest the assertion that warnings were given. In the language of philosophy, this can be termed coherence, as the point is to establish the truth of a statement not in itself, by comparing it with the facts it articulates, but on the basis of other evidence that helps to substantiate it. However, this evidence can also be contested: the weapon could have been placed next to the body by the gendarmes to pretend that they had been assaulted, and the denial that there were any warnings might result from an agreement between the members of the family to incriminate the officers.

In the absence of cameras that would allow certain facts to be verified, magistrates and investigators thus cannot know irrefutably which of the versions, the gendarmes' or the family's, is true purely on the basis either of correspondence between the statements and the facts or of coherence between the statements and other evidence. However, while in principle magistrates and investigators seem to face unresolvable situations, in practice it is clear that they form an opinion that rapidly tends to become a firm conviction. As early as the day after the tragedy, the public prosecutor gives a press conference in which he reiterates the gendarmes' version, without mentioning the family's account. Similarly, a week after the events, the General Inspectorate of the Gendarmerie publishes a report asserting that there appears to be no contradiction between the depositions of the officers who fired and the various testimonies gathered, once again ignoring the statements of the victim's family. The final sentence in both the press conference and investigation report, to the effect that further expert examination must be awaited to draw final conclusions, seems a necessary but unconvincing rhetorical caveat. One indication of this is that the ballistic data, which do not support the gendarmes' accounts, and are available the day after the tragedy, are not taken up to question their version and, on the contrary, are provided to the GIGN to facilitate the re-enactment. The public prosecutor and the gendarmerie inspectors have already decided what the truth is. It is unlikely that new evidence will modify their assessment. Hence the surprise when the examining magistrate decides to place the officers under investigation.

The process whereby the public prosecutor and the criminal investigation officers initially form this judgment consists of three strands: reduction of the discrepancies between the gendarmes' versions, exclusion of the contradictory testimony of the family, and selection from among the available information. First, the substantial variations between the versions of the five men are erased. The fact that the first officer says the individual was silent while the second describes him yelling abuse, that the second speaks of a knife while the first says he did not see it – these differences, and many others, are eliminated. What remains is a smooth, homogeneous account. Second, the serious contradictions between this account and the family's version are disregarded. The fact that five individuals who were located very close to the annex testify that, in the seconds preceding the rounds of semi-automatic pistol fire, they heard no sound of a confrontation, nor any kind of warning, disappears from the description of the sequence of events leading to the death. The word of the family vanishes. Third, a choice is made from among the evidence to validate the interpretation of events. For example, the presence of a knife is taken into account, without questioning the fact that it was found in line with the arm, although the body had been moved and turned over, inverting the position of the right hand; and while the bullet-hole in the ceiling is mentioned, the bullet paths in the body, which contradict the gendarmes' assertions, are not. This threefold process of analysis of the facts thus results in the account that appears obvious to the public prosecutor, the criminal investigation officers and, later, the examining magistrate.

How is this process of selecting among testimonies and evidence to be accounted for, and, more generally, in the absence of evidence that can guarantee certainty, what is the mechanism that leads someone to favor one interpretation of the facts over another? Sociologists suggest two main explanations, which are to some extent related: the hierarchy of credibility and the power of affinity. On the one hand, magistrates and investigators tend to believe certain people more easily than others. They set up mentally a hierarchy of the faith they place in different parties, on the basis of criteria that may be explicit and juridical, for example when one of the parties has sworn an oath of office and the other has not, or implicit and affective, particularly when there is a climate of prejudice in favor of or against one or the other party. In this case the two types of criteria come together. The gendarmes have been sworn in. The Travellers are subject to negative prejudices. The credit accorded to the former combines with the discredit of the latter. On the other hand, magistrates and investigators develop elective relationships with certain groups and strong antagonism toward others. The public prosecutor works daily with the gendarmes, who represent a sort of essential auxiliary, since they provide them with criminal cases to examine and arrest the alleged perpetrators. The criminal investigation officers are in the singular position of questioning colleagues. The two officers who fired thus belong to the institutional world of the former and the professional world of the latter. Conversely, there is a considerable social and also psychological distance between judges and Travellers. The varying degrees of contempt of professionals in the justice system, which may be manifested as condescension, sarcasm or aggressiveness, are met by the general hostility of the Travellers, who have developed a deep mistrust of the penal system through their many interactions with it. Thus the hierarchy of credibility and the power of affinity are so inculcated in the magistrates and investigators that they tend, one might almost say quite naturally, to favor the version of the gendarmes over that of the family to the extent of completely ignoring the latter, regardless of the plausibility of either one and the discrepancies and corroborations on either side. And even, it can be supposed, without any intention to distort the facts: they may be convinced that they are analyzing a situation in all conscience.

Ultimately, given contradictory statements about what actually happened, and in the absence of definitive evidence confirming one version or the other, as in this case, the answer to the question: What is truth? is not to be sought either in correspondence between accounts and facts or in coherence between accounts and evidence. From a sociological point of view, in the final analysis, truth is what the majority of members of a society hold to be true. When the case is processed through the justice system, the only version that counts, the one that will be retained, is the one accepted by the courts. It is on this truth that the decision to convict some and exonerate others is based. The magistrates and investigators do not even need to believe it. What matters is that they articulate it. For it is this truth that is retained by history. In this sense the justice system has a performative role, as philosophers of language have shown. What it says comes to be, simply through the act of articulation. The decision it makes becomes truth. Attacked by a raving maniac, the officers fired at him in legitimate self-defense. The truth sanctioned by the justice system, and adopted by the media as the official truth, is contained in this single phrase. And it is because they know that the justice system has this performative power that Angelo's family fight in the hope, perennially dashed, that it might recognize a different version of the circumstances of his death and at last bring this version into existence as the truth in the eyes of the world.

In his press conference the day after the tragedy, the public prosecutor spoke of what he called his first duty in this case: To get as close as possible to the truth. He added, with lucidity: Which will be the judicial truth.

XVI
Lies

They are often thought of as the opposite of truth, but they should in fact be contrasted with sincerity. A lie is a statement which one knows to be false and addresses to others with the intention of making them believe that it is true. It may be difficult to expose. Those who are lying know that they are doing so, but the persons they are talking to are supposed not to know. Even if they suspect it, it is usually difficult for them to prove it. In this case, while the public prosecutor thinks that the family is lying and that they did indeed hear the gendarmes' warnings and the uproar of a confrontation, it will be difficult for him to demonstrate; if the examining magistrate thinks that the officers are lying and in fact fired without warning at an unarmed man, she will find this hard to establish. But, like the search for truth, exposing a lie is an unequal process. In the justice system, some who lie are more likely than others not to be found out, thanks to their status and social resources.

This is especially the case with the police or, as in the present case, the gendarmerie, for a number of reasons. First, they are sworn officers of the law, and therefore supposed to lie less than others, and, what is more, they find themselves facing other representatives of sworn professions, such as prosecutors, judges and lawyers. Second, they develop an *esprit de corps* that almost invariably leads them to support the accounts of their colleagues suspected of committing a wrongful act. Finally, external witnesses to this act who could thus expose the lie cannot get their voice to be heard, either because their testimony is not registered or because it receives less attention during the investigation proceedings. International criminological studies have long since observed these mechanisms. And there is no shortage of recent examples confirming them, through the revelations of an audio or video recording, a journalist's investigation of an incident, or simply the belated confession of a repentant officer. These three reasons offer a general explanation of why the lies of the police are effective when they are charged. They do not of course predict whether, in specific cases involving one of their own, officers are lying or not, but they help to understand why, if they lie, it is particularly difficult to counter them.

There are situations when lies prove especially necessary to law-enforcement agents. These are the situations of what are commonly called blunders but should more properly be termed simply violence. When brutality is perpetrated by gendarmes or police officers, the agents concerned, their colleagues and their superiors are easily tempted to conceal it or at least to dress up the circumstances in such a way as to make it legally acceptable and hence not subject to criminal sanction. Legitimate self-defense is the argument most often used, and the law of 28 February 2017 extended the scope of application of this claim, making it easier to invoke it, since it permitted recourse to armed force specifically against escaped persons or vehicles who refuse to stop and might make attempts on the life or bodily integrity of police officers or others; this effectively amounts to authorizing officers to shoot a fugitive or any supposedly dangerous person.

The lie works all the better if it is supported by consistent testimony from witnesses. Moreover, the recourse to a collective lie in cases of violence, particularly when it has led to the death of an individual, presents several advantages for police officers. First, it constitutes an efficacious defense, making it possible to exonerate the perpetrators; the mildness of internal sanctions and the rarity of court convictions of officers directly or indirectly involved in the death of individuals are well documented. Second, it helps to reinforce solidarity within the group, since the witnesses show solidarity by adding their mendacious words to those of their colleagues directly involved, and all are then bound in a sort of secret pact by the violation of their oath. Third, it protects the institution from the risk of damage to its public image, which partly explains why senior officers and even politicians, up to the highest level of government, are so ready to contribute to concealing the truth. It should be added that, in the rare cases where officers report abuses committed by their colleagues to their superiors, it is they who find themselves sanctioned. Here, again, both criminological studies and contemporary cases offer copious theoretical analysis and empirical evidence of these mechanisms of collective lying.

To be sure, it could be argued that lying to an investigator or magistrate to avoid a penalty is understandable and normal. Indeed, the Fifth Amendment to the Constitution of the United States protects the accused from the obligation to testify against themselves. But, in the case of law-enforcement agents, lying has a significance different from lying by ordinary citizens. In the case of ordinary citizens, these are individual lies. For the police or the gendarmes, the lies are institutional, in other words incorporated into the core of the organization to protect it against inquiries and sanctions. Just as we speak of institutional racism when we consider discrimination, so we should speak of institutional duplicity when we reflect on lying.

The falsification of the facts when violence has been perpetrated can even go beyond exoneration of the perpetrators. It can serve at the same time to incriminate the victims. This is facilitated by the offense of insulting and resisting a person invested with public authority, which has seen increasing use in France over the last thirty years. The perpetrator of violence accuses the person who has been subjected to it, claiming that the abusive and aggressive behavior of the individual concerned made it necessary to use force. In some cases, there may be a negotiated joint withdrawal of both complaints, as the victim of violence comes to understand the unfavorable balance of power in the judicial context. In others, the two complaints are pursued, but the judge is generally more sensitive to the offense allegedly perpetrated against officers as the political climate and legislative developments support ever greater severity toward this offense. Specious recourse to the offense of insulting and resisting a person invested with authority in order to sweep violence perpetrated by officers under the carpet is a well-known police tactic among both rank-and-file officers and their superiors, and even extending to some high-ranking public security officials, to the extent that, for police chiefs, a high level of frequency of this offense is deemed an indicator of officers' aggressiveness. It is thus clear that, given all of these practices taken together, victims of police violence have very little chance of seeing the harm done to them recognized and their rights upheld.

In the United States, the institutionalization of false testimony is such a common phenomenon that there is a police slang term that demonstrates how routine and even acceptable it has become: testilying, a hybrid word that combines testifying and lying. It designates a practice defined in law as police perjury, but legal scholars and police chiefs agree that it is quite standard, whether the aim is to protect officers or incriminate suspects. Studies show that, while citizen grand juries tasked with deciding whether the alleged perpetrators of a crime should be indicted respond affirmatively in ninety-nine percent of cases of homicide committed by an ordinary citizen, they return a negative response in ninety-nine percent of cases where a police officer kills an individual, even unarmed.

The fact that grand jury hearings and discussions take place under the guidance of the prosecutor, who works in close collaboration with the police, depending on them for cases and arrests of suspects, is not unconnected to this statistic. However, the increasingly frequent requirement in the United States that police officers wear body cameras during their operations could reduce, if not the risk of false testimony, at least the probability that they will prevail in court. Such devices are not used in France.

In the case of the operation that ended in Angelo's death, body cameras would surely have made it possible to know what really happened in the shed. The questions asked by the criminal investigation officers suggest that it would have been desirable for the gendarmes to be equipped with them. Wearing them might even also have modified their behavior throughout the operation. There is a hint of this in the way they present their actions in their statements. Not only do they use strictly technical and apparently neutral language, speaking of processing buildings, handling individuals, and moving away from the objective, but some, startlingly, even describe their attitude to members of the family as friendly and benevolent. The officer who fired the first series of shots, in particular, stresses the care he took with them. He describes how considerate he was when he detained the son and how carefully he put the soft handcuffs on him. He states that a little while later he reassured the father, whom he was briefly guarding, telling him that everything would be fine. These surprising descriptions contrast not only with the accounts of shouted commands, brutality and humiliation as reported by Angelo's family, and suggested by the injuries they exhibited during their depositions, but also with the entirety of the intervention procedure as described by the other gendarmes: the look of the men in balaclavas, kitted out with shields and helmets; the use of heavy weapons, including submachine guns and semi-automatic pistols; the pinning down and holding of the men on the ground at gunpoint. Given subsequent events as far as this officer is concerned, this apparent embellishment seems designed to create a positive image of his behavior, so that he is less likely to be suspected of acting nervously and aggressively.

Be that as it may, lying is rarely a gratuitous act, particularly when it is done collectively. There is a rationality behind lying. Generally, people lie when they have an interest in doing so, either to protect themselves or to protect persons close to them. This is particularly true when there is a possibility of sanction. Thus, the father, mother and uncle assert, in their first statements, that they did not know Angelo was on their property. This is false, and they do subsequently amend their testimony. But there is a clear benefit for them in maintaining this claim at a point when, in shock after the events, they do not know what they risk for having harbored a family member deemed a fugitive, particularly given that they have been treated like dangerous criminals by gendarmes in combat gear who held them captive for several hours. To demonstrate his respect for the law, the father even states that he had spoken to his son on the telephone a little while before and advised him to return to prison, which in fact appears to be true. The false story about Angelo's presence at their home is clumsy, but there is a reason for it: what the public prosecutor calls their loyalty.

As far as the events in the lean-to are concerned, the interest the two sides have in lying differs. It is easy to divine the motives leading the two officers who fired at Angelo, their comrades who were there with them, and even their superiors located outside to distort the truth. For the two who fired, if it was established that they had fired for reasons other than legitimate self-defense, they would be convicted in court; for their fellow officers, failing to stand with their colleagues would be seen as a serious breach of unity; for the senior officers, violation of the rules of engagement and responsibility for a homicide would lead to inquiries into the grounds for and tactics of the intervention, unleash a public outcry, and

ultimately tarnish the image of the GIGN. Conversely, the
probability that the falsehood will be discovered is minute.
The risk–benefit ratio of presenting a false account is thus
heavily in their favor. By contrast, it is hard to see what
motives could lead Angelo's family to falsify the events
they witnessed by claiming that they heard no sound after
the gendarmes entered the shed, to invent an officer calling
for them to hold fire and use stun grenades, and to imagine
muttered discussions among the GIGN men following the
shots. From a rational point of view, lying is more logical
on one side than on the other. Which does not prove that
those who had an interest in lying did so or that those who
did not have such an interest did not.

But lying is not just a problem of rationality, it is also
a question of morality. In philosophy, two opposing con-
ceptions of ethics have been argued for over two centuries.
According to the first, known as the consequentialist
theory, the moral rightness of an act is judged on the basis
of the effects it produces. Lying can therefore be justified if
the repercussions of the lie are overall positive. According
to the second, deontological theory, the moral rightness of
an act is judged on the basis of its conformity with moral
obligations, irrespective of its consequences. Lying is therefore always reprehensible because it is a failure to respect
the obligation to tell the truth. From a deontological perspective, the gendarmes therefore must not lie, particularly
as they are sworn not to do so. But from a consequentialist
point of view, they may think that, even if the version they
present to the magistrates and investigators is false, saying
that Angelo was armed and that they gave warnings before
they fired avoids pointless collateral damage, including a
painful ordeal for their own families if they are convicted
and potential harm to the institution as the trial of the two
officers would certainly become also a trial of the GIGN;
they may feel all the more that it is acceptable if they can
persuade themselves that this will change nothing for their
victim. Thus, the gendarmes could find moral justification
for falsifying the events. By contrast, if the family lied,

the sole satisfaction of unwarranted revenge on the police would be unacceptable from the consequentialist point of view, because it is difficult to consider this satisfaction to be a positive effect, while in deontological terms such an act would be doubly reprehensible with regard to the truth that it would traduce and the justice that it would betray at the very moment the family is demanding both. It is hard for them to find a justification for altering the truth. There is therefore an asymmetry of positions with regard to the morality of lying. But here, again, the fact that the gendarmes could think they were acting morally by not telling the truth while the family could not is no predictor of what actually happened.

There is a final, rarely discussed aspect to lying: its relation to the sacred. When they swear their oath, the gendarmes are probably not aware that the French word for oath, *serment*, shares its Latin etymology with the word sacrament, and that it originally meant a promise or an affirmation made before God, or a sacred being or object. In its contemporary, secular version it is no longer anything more than a prosaic obedience to a boss and proper use of force. By contrast, for Travellers, the taboo of the sacred seems to retain its power in some specific circumstances. We have a principle, says Angelo's younger sister. We never lie about someone's death.

XVII

Reconstruction

Strictly speaking, it never took place. There was, to be sure, a re-enactment with the gendarmes on the day after the events in the presence of the public prosecutor and the investigators, but it was conducted in the absence of the five witnesses from the family. There was also, six months later, a visit to the location by the examining magistrate in the presence of a representative of the prosecutor's office and gendarmerie inspectors, but the focus was mainly on verifying the layout of the property and how voices carried between the lean-to where the killing took place and the patio where the family was. In the end, it was decided that the material in the case file was sufficient to determine what decision should be made with regard to the two officers placed under investigation – that is, whether the case should be dismissed or referred to court. A judicial reconstruction, which is not automatically part of the investigation procedure, was not deemed necessary. The case was dismissed. The ruling was confirmed on appeal. Justice was dispensed.

So, if there was no point in a judicial reconstruction, can a different reconstruction be imagined – one conducted with the aim not of dispensing justice but of doing justice? Dispensing justice is the role of the judicial system. Its work is essential to democracy, but many studies have shown that it often fails to uphold the principle of equal treatment of all parties, both in the amount of attention paid and resources deployed and in the procedures conducted and sanctions issued. Doing justice, on the contrary, consists of an attempt to re-establish some kind of equity by ascribing equal value to each party. In the case of Angelo's death, the investigators from the General Inspectorate of the Gendarmerie did not point out how the family's testimony contradicted the officers' version, and nor did the public prosecutor take this up. At the very beginning of the procedure, the words of Angelo's family were disregarded, just as their presence at the re-enactment was deemed unnecessary. Doing them justice means not only listening to what they have to say but also recognizing that what they have to say about the death of their son, brother and nephew has the same worth as what the gendarmes may have said about it. This is an ethical requirement.

A different form of reconstruction logically follows from this principle of equal treatment. It involves gathering together all of the material in the case file and considering it without presuming that the words of some parties should be given more credit than others, that some contradictions do not require the same scrutiny as others, that some lines of evidence are of less interest than others. It also presupposes listening to what the protagonists may say at some distance from the events, during depositions or interviews, and taking this into account with no other aim than that of doing justice to each of them. An attempt is made here to put the pieces of the puzzle together.

The version of the five members of the family present at the scene is both simple and consistent. A noise is heard from the shed just as the gendarmes have finished searching the premises. Several of them move toward the small annex. A few seconds after they have entered, a series of shots ring out. In that brief interval, no sound has been heard apart from the men moving about inside. No indication of a confrontation, no shouts from the victim, no orders from the gendarmes. Just the sounds of footsteps and people banging into objects. And right after the shots, a groan that some of them hear. Then someone, probably a senior officer, runs up shouting to hold fire and use grenades. After that there is a moment of muffled conversation in the lean-to. A gendarme comes out, holding a blood-stained cloth that the father and sister-in-law recognize as Angelo's tee-shirt. Two others appear soon after, carrying a third fellow officer who is apparently concussed but whom the family see getting up a little too swiftly in the courtyard. While they question the gendarmes to find out what has happened, they are moved away from the site of the events to the garden wall. The only – short-lived – variation in this account comes from the sister-in-law's first statement, made four hours after the tragedy, in what she will subsequently describe as a state of shock. She first says that she heard only objects falling in the lumber room after the gendarmes entered, then, when she is instructed to repeat her account, she mentions the shouts of someone who could have been Angelo, but she is not asked to specify the exact timing, in particular whether it came before or after the officers fired. When she is later deposed by the judge, she nevertheless asserts that she heard neither the gendarmes nor her brother-in-law in the brief moment before the shots.

The GIGN men's version is also clear and coherent – at least in its basic form. The common framework is as follows. In the context of a systematic search of the premises where the man they are seeking to arrest might be hiding, two gendarmes enter a lumber room adjacent to the main residence, followed by three others. They find the man they call the objective there and announce their presence to him. As they try to seize him, one of them realizes that he has a knife and warns his colleagues. They draw back to protect themselves but the man rushes toward them, threatening them with his knife. Two shots from an electric pulse gun fail to stop him. Seeing the man about to stab his comrade, one of the officers fires, then is thrown backward and fires once more. A second, just behind him, seeing the man lunge toward him while his colleague is on the floor, fires in his turn. The individual falls forward. He is turned onto his back and handcuffed. Assistance is called for the two injured men. It is rapidly discovered that the man is dead. The handcuffs are then removed. The officer who fell is evacuated, still stunned. In the courtyard his protective gear is removed and he gets up again. An initial reconstruction is carried out in the lean-to with the unit captain, followed by another in the courtyard. The elite unit gathers for debriefing.

But the statements from the gendarmes, particularly those taken on the evening of Angelo's death, reveal substantial variations and even imply contradictions that are difficult to reconcile. However, these are not taken up, either in the report by the criminal investigation officers or in the public prosecutor's statements or the examining magistrate's ruling. Let us consider the testimonies given by each in relation to two crucial moments: when Angelo was discovered and during the confrontation.

At the moment when he is discovered, a first gendarme asserts that he sees an individual curled into a ball and that he asks him to raise his hands, which the man does immediately, staying in this position for a moment without moving, even though he is then ordered to come forward. The second officer, who stands at his side, states that, when he is revealed by the laser light, the man turns to face them, gesticulates, shouts, abuses them and refuses to obey the repeated command to lie on the ground. The first officer, who is just behind his two colleagues, says that he arrived a few seconds after the objective was found but maintains that the man did not utter a sound at any point in the intervention. A second gendarme hears his comrades tell the individual to come forward as he is standing in front of them, in a boxing stance with raised fists. The third gendarme offers hardly any details. In short, during the first moments of the interaction with the gendarmes, was Angelo motionless or agitated? Was he yelling or silent?

Did he raise his hands in the air or hold up his fists? And was he ordered to get up, to lie down or to come forward?

During the confrontation, the first gendarme recounts that, as he moves to seize the individual, the man puts up a struggle and pulls out a knife, making sweeping gestures in front of him. A first taser shot by one of his colleagues does not shake him, nor does his own, and he sees him pull out the darts embedded in his body. Swerving away from a knife thrust, he falls with his assailant and, as he ends up lying alongside him on the floor, manages to seize his wrist and make him let go of the knife. As he fell he heard gunshots. According to the second officer, he is the one who tries to bring the individual under control without using a weapon but stops when he hears his comrade call out that there is a knife. He sees two electrodes penetrate the torso of the crazed individual, who flies into an uncontrollable rage. He discerns the man trying to stab his colleague in the throat, fires a first time, takes a blow on the chin without knowing who has hit him and falls backward; then, as he is lying on the floor, he sees the individual still standing and fires a second time before he loses consciousness. The first officer, for his part, does not describe any attempt to seize the man and does not see him with a knife at any point, even wondering if he is not actually carrying a handgun. He fires a taser shot, and the crazed man tries to pull out the cables. He recounts that the individual lunges at his colleagues, that one of them falls backward, that the other is dragged toward the wall, that shots are fired and someone shouts: I'm hit!, which he interprets as an injury to one of his comrades. When he sees the man moving toward him, threatening, he fires point blank. Blood gushes and the individual collapses. The second gendarme reports that he approaches the objective and tries unsuccessfully to take him by the shoulder. The man first remains in his initial position, still making circular gestures with his weapon, then makes a faint movement forward. Two taser shots hit him but he pulls out the cables. Gunshots ring out, but he continues to walk toward the gendarmes with his knife out. Eventually he collapses. Finally, the third gendarme sees the first and second try to grab hold of the target, who pushes them away and pulls out his blade. Impervious to the two taser shots, whose cables he pulls out, the man approaches the gendarmes and tries to cut them with circular movements. Someone opens fire as he is still moving forward. They all fall to the ground, including the individual. The confrontation is described as like a rugby scrum.

So what actually happened at this crucial moment? Even if we ignore the minor variations, such as the fact that all except one saw two taser shots and all except another saw the cables pulled out – details of which the investigators nevertheless take note during the depositions – there are other troubling elements. How could the officer who fired the allegedly fatal shot never have seen the knife, when he describes the man advancing aggressively toward him? Could someone really have shouted: I'm hit!, as he says, when four out of the five gendarmes did not hear it? Was it one, two or three of them who grabbed hold of their target before he pulled out his weapon? And did one, two or four of them end up on the floor at the end of the sequence? Lastly, did Angelo collapse immediately after receiving the *coup de grâce*, as the officer who fired facing him and thinks he fatally wounded him says, or did he continue to struggle when he had fallen to the ground, wrestling with the gendarmes as they tried to seize his weapon from him, as two of his colleagues claim?

How are these variations in the accounts to be interpreted? The scene is supposed to be played out over a very short period of time in an emotionally charged situation. Under such circumstances memories can become confused. But while psychologists confirm the existence of false memories, particularly in relation to traumatic events, these might rather be expected on the side of the family, who have just lost a loved one, than that of the gendarmes, particularly those not involved in the death. And here the opposite is the case. Equally noteworthy is

the fact that the criminal investigation officers left these
discrepancies virtually unexplored during the depositions
and that the subsequent court decisions made no mention of them, particularly given that there are manifest
contradictions regarding elements that are relatively easily
differentiated. The same lack of curiosity is apparent in the
short depositions of the members of the family, when the
investigators simply accept their assertion that there were
no warnings before the shots, a fact that the gendarmes
themselves acknowledge, without asking them to state
specifically whether they also did not hear orders issued by
the GIGN men, the shouts of the young man, or any other
noises suggesting a fight. As to the fact that the individual
killed is described by the gendarmes as bare-chested, while
the family state categorically that he entered the lean-to
wearing a tee-shirt, describe him as sensitive to cold and
therefore very unlikely to undress in a chilly lumber room
in early spring, and two of them assert that they saw a
gendarme come out holding a bloody garment which then
disappeared, this is not explored in any way.

But the accounts of the family and of the gendarmes
are of course not the only data available as a basis for
forming a firm opinion. Alongside the question of whether
the facts are true, there is the issue of whether they are
plausible. The examining magistrate appears to imply that
she has doubts about this when the gendarmes first appear
before her and she asks them if they do not think there is
a disproportion between the threat of a lone individual
armed with a pocket knife in a confined space and the
intervention of five men carrying tasers, submachine guns
and semi-automatic pistols, who fire eight times. Above
and beyond the disproportion, the plausibility of the
claim is itself in question, as the lawyer representing the
family emphasizes, for it requires imagining that a man
armed only with a four-inch knife would attack five over-
equipped gendarmes, heavily armed with submachine
guns and semi-automatic pistols and protected by helmets
and bulletproof vests. Credibility might also have been

disputed in relation to the astonishing reactions of the allegedly crazed man to the tens of thousands of volts of taser charge, which normally have the effect of blocking the nervous system and causing temporary paralysis, occasionally death, and which in this case produce only a brief spasm followed by renewed vigor. But it is clear why it is important to the gendarmes that the possibility of such supraphysiological reactions, even in a man of slight build who had suffered lasting pain in his ribs from a previous taser shot, should not be challenged, since the taser shots help to establish the grounds for the final recourse to semi-automatic pistols: the gradual escalation of the response. While neither the implausibility of the victim attacking five GIGN men on his own nor the improbability of such a reaction to a powerful electric charge is sufficient to invalidate the gendarmes' version, the conjunction of the two is, to say the least, troubling.

An examination of the facts aimed at reconstructing the sequence of events must also take into account the evidence that is independent both of the testimony of the protagonists, who may always be suspected of being biased if not lying, and of the assessment of the investigators as to the plausibility or otherwise of certain facts. It is certainly remarkable that the scene of the tragedy was not placed under seal, that the gendarmes were able to spend more time there, and that the position of items in the lean-to was, by their own admission, altered. Despite this carelessness of the investigation, various objective elements were gathered, some of them by default. At the medical examination carried out on the evening of the events, the first gendarme, who states that he received an attack to the neck, shows no clinical sign on his upper body, not even a scratch, while the second officer, who describes being thrown backward by a violent blow to the chin, shows no visible trace of this assault, not even a bruise. Both have grazes, but these are on their limbs. Furthermore, the forensic report records the presence of a knife in line with the victim's right hand, a few inches away, a position that suggests it has just been released, when the first officer, who asserts that he never saw the weapon at any point during the confrontation, states that he moved the body and turned it over for the sake of dignity, thus reversing the positions of the right and left arms. Is it even certain that the knife was really used in the lean-to? The emergency doctor's radio call to his colleague in dispatch invites doubt, since he states that the guy was not armed, adding that he has expressly been requested to maintain complete discretion. Of course, this is ultimately only hearsay repeated by the doctor, but the discomfort he shows during his deposition reinforces doubt as to the knife attack.

Two other pieces of objective evidence perhaps merit closer attention: the autopsy, supplemented by ballistic data, and the forensic examination of the tasers. As already noted, the autopsy reveals the existence of five wounds in the thorax, with the bullet paths all on a steep angle from above to below, more than forty-five degrees to the horizontal and in one case almost vertical. They therefore imply that those who fired the fatal shots were well above the victim and also probably very close. One of the officers, however, asserts that he fired at the target standing in front of him and then once more when he was on the ground, while the other claims that he was also facing him. This would imply horizontal or upward bullet paths, contrary to the autopsy and ballistic data. With regard to the tasers, the recorded time of the shots from the electric pulse guns shows what initially appears to be a surprising gap of nearly seven minutes. Synchronization in the lab reveals that, with regard to the correct time, one of the two was fast and the other slow. Yet even taking this double correction into account, there is still a significant gap of nine seconds between the two discharges. The gendarmes describe the tasers being discharged one after the other, as might be imagined given the violence of the alleged attack, since those who fired the fatal shots suggest that things moved so fast they had no time to give warnings before they fired. The forensic examination also shows that the taser belonging to the officer who remembers firing second was discharged before that of his comrade, who asserts that he fired first. Although the autopsy data and the taser measurements are cited in the ruling dismissing the case, neither of the corresponding discrepancies is discussed in the document's conclusions.

As is customary, the role of the justice system in this case is limited to determining whether those placed under investigation for violence with use of a weapon leading to involuntary homicide should be indicted and, if they are, whether or not they should be convicted. If the judicial reconstruction had taken place it would therefore have been confined to the lean-to and the events that took place there, and it was indeed within these limits that the actual investigation was, quite logically, conducted.

However, the sociological reconstruction must go beyond these bounds and situate what was played out when the shots were fired in a broader context. What is at issue in this tragedy cannot only be the question of whether the two officers who killed Angelo did so in legitimate self-defense or whether they committed a crime in yielding to panic when they discovered the man they had come to arrest. It must also be to understand the circumstances that led to an operation mobilizing two dozen gendarmes in assault formation for the arrest of a man whose main crimes consisted of driving without a license and non-violent thefts, and whom a sentence enforcement judge had assessed as a low enough risk to give him home leave from prison two-thirds of the way through his sentence.

One police officer told a national newspaper journalist that he thought the GIGN intervention was actually a training exercise. However, this is merely conjecture. More certain is the fact that, with the proliferation of special police units theoretically tasked with intervening in extreme situations such as terrorist attacks or hostage situations, their threshold for intervention is in fact becoming lower, because their existence leads to their being deployed well beyond the exceptional circumstances for which they were created. Even if Angelo's arrest was not explicitly designed as a GIGN training exercise, it manifests the tendency to call on them without hesitation for increasingly routine operations. Since they exist, they have to be put to use, and fortunately terrorist attacks and hostage-taking are rare. Thus, they are entrusted with interventions on relatively minor targets. This same logic prevails in the spreading deployment of BAC, anti-crime squads, in low-income neighborhoods, and in the increasingly routine use of ERIS, regional intervention and security teams, in prisons. As in the United States, where it reaches new heights with the integration of military weaponry into internal security, the militarization of the police, with its SWAT teams, which the GIGN resembles, is being normalized, leading to operations on a disproportionate scale.

But this development is not evenly distributed through society. The question it raises is that of the conditions of possibility of such a disproportionate and eventually lethal intervention. The testimony of all the gendarmes involved in this operation confirms that the fact the arrest concerned a Traveller was a determining factor in the judicial decision to call on the GIGN rather than less aggressive gendarmerie units. First, because individuals described thus are generally seen as in principle dangerous and feared in a way that is quite irrational, given that only in exceptional cases do they attack people outside of their own community, still less law-enforcement officers, especially when they are settled and well known to the local police. Second, because the gendarmes know that, even when they do abuse their authority during an intervention with this community, there will be no consequences, as demonstrated by the fact that the humiliation of the family and the destructive search of their residence gave rise to neither apology nor compensation. It is thus the denigration, stigmatization and marginalization of Travellers that makes possible what would be unimaginable in other social contexts. The racism toward them that permeates the whole of society is the ultimate sociological cause of Angelo's death, just as much as the fatal shots. The weight of this tragedy therefore does not rest solely on the shoulders of the two officers, whether they are exonerated, as the judges decided, or sanctioned, as the family demand.

However, since the ruling dismissing the case against them was constructed by disregarding the inconsistencies and discrepancies in testimony, the factual implausibilities, the procedural failures and the disturbing evidence, it is important to re-examine the grounds on which it was based. Or, rather, to re-examine the account that underlies it. Would it in fact not be possible to conceive of another account that reintegrated these elements and grasped their significance? Because, taken together, they make sense. What was incomprehensible, absurd, strange, contradictory in the version of events presented as judicial truth can, through a reconstruction taking into account only the facts, become intelligible and meaningful again. Let us, therefore, imagine another version of what might have happened on the day of Angelo's death.

XVIII
That Day

The first officer hears the telephone ring. Looks at his alarm clock. It's ten. He has slept only four hours. He is on call this week and there had been an intervention during the night – the arrest of four individuals at a house one hundred and twenty miles from their base. Drug dealers. The mission went according to plan. He gets up, dresses quickly and joins his unit, who are in the process of gathering. He learns that this new operation concerns a man who has escaped from prison in the region. He belongs to the travelling community. He has been located at his parents' farm. The GIGN has been called because the man is reputed to be dangerous, perhaps armed. His arrest is deemed to go beyond the scope of the surveillance and intervention team whose job it would normally be. There is a briefing. They are shown a photo of the fugitive and of his son, who are traveling together in a white vehicle. A plan of the farm is projected, with the location of caravans and the identities of the residents. They are given brief instructions on the methods to be used in the intervention, as it is important not to risk the individual leaving the site before they arrive. The first officer wonders: Isn't it a bit disproportionate to call in the GIGN to arrest a gypsy? If the guy had home leave, he can't be that dangerous.

The gendarmes kit themselves out with their heavy protective gear and sophisticated assault weapons. All have a bulletproof vest, a helmet with visor, a semi-automatic pistol with laser sight, and stun grenades. The rest of their equipment varies, depending on their position in the different groups. Some have a shield, others a portable radio and first-aid kit, others pump-action shotguns, submachine guns or tasers. The first officer, who has completed explosives training, carries a battering ram. The total weight of the gendarmes' kit can be nearly ninety pounds.

The operation begins. Fifteen or so gendarmes cram into the back of an unmarked truck. In the cab at the front, three of their team in plain clothes, caps turned backward. Incognito. The van is really uncomfortable for a journey that takes more than an hour. Along the way the driver notes that roadblocks have started to be put in place. When they get to the location they are told that the plan has changed because there is only one occupant in the vehicle parked by the farm. It will be a bit more complicated. On reaching the gate, the truck stops. The gendarmes clamber out silently. Two of them easily detain the teenager sitting in the car, who nevertheless tries to warn his family, shouting: The cops! They handcuff him and make him lie down beside the road. Four others go off to take position around the perimeter of the property. The rest of them gather in groups of three and burst into the courtyard shouting: Police! Several gendarmes rush toward the four residents present, yelling orders: three men and a woman in the process of preparing a barbecue. They kick the men to the ground, restrain them with soft handcuffs and hold them down with a boot in the back. They order the woman to kneel with her hands on her head; she is soon joined by another who was further away in her caravan and whom they didn't see when they came in. They hold them all under guard at gunpoint. The situation is under control. The prisoners protest vociferously. The man who looks to be the father, a tube in his nose, obviously short of breath, demands his oxygen. The woman who must be his wife, unsteady, complains that she is in pain. They are told to shut up. A young child contemplates the scene, dumbstruck. A gendarme tells him to go to bed.

During this time, all the residences are searched, following the pre-planned deployment of the teams. From top to bottom, beds lifted, wardrobes emptied, furniture moved. The first officer takes on the caravans with two of his colleagues. The other teams explore the buildings. The objective is nowhere to be found. Could he have had time to flee out back, toward the little wood that lies only a few dozen yards beyond the fence? Obviously there's no way they will get any information out of the family. The gendarmes who have finished searching the premises gather in the middle of the courtyard to decide what to do next. After the din of the first minutes of the intervention, a kind of calm seems to have returned. The parents have finally stopped complaining and asking questions. The gendarmes discuss how to proceed. Suddenly they are alerted by a sound. It comes from an annex to the main building, to which they have paid no attention until now. Two of them move in that direction. The first officer decides to go after them. Two other gendarmes follow him.

The two GIGN men enter the lumber room, submachine guns in hand. In the darkness, they can make out nothing but a jumble of objects cluttering the floor and blocking their path. The second officer changes his weapon. He puts away his heavy gun and takes out his semi-automatic pistol, lighting its laser sight. The beam sweeps the store. Crates, tools, old furniture. He advances with difficulty amid the clutter, stumbling over cardboard boxes. Moving in this environment with such a heavy kit is anything but easy. Behind him, the first officer has entered, followed by two other gendarmes. All three have their semi-automatic pistols in hand. Suddenly the light illuminates a silhouette huddled into a recess against the back wall, barely a yard in front of them. Realizing that he has been discovered, the man raises his hands in the air and begins to stand up. Surprised, the second officer starts when he sees him so close. He cannot control his reaction. He fires. Several bullets into the chest. Trips on an obstacle, falls backward, knocks into his colleague, fires again. Behind him, the first officer has not understood what was happening. He fires in his turn. A single bullet. Almost point blank. A reflex. The man collapses. He utters a short groan. Outside, someone yells to hold fire. Maybe use a stun grenade to make the target come out. Too late. The individual has been hit. Seriously. Everything happened so fast. Just a few seconds.

With the help of one of his comrades, the first officer pulls the man up and handcuffs him, mechanically. This is the routine in an arrest. The guy seems to be unconscious. His tee-shirt is soaked with blood. His vital functions are failing. But it does not occur to anyone to resuscitate him. The second officer gets up. He has picked up some scratches in falling. In the gloom he can just make out the man lying at his feet. He feels stunned, less from the fall than from the awareness of what his action has just brought about. The first officer also appears at a loss. It is the first time he has drawn his weapon to fire at someone. He calls for help over the radio. The major enters the lean-to. He asks if there are any casualties, discovers the dying man and, seeing the dismayed gendarmes, guesses what has just happened. He makes a rapid assessment of the situation. It does not look good. A lone, unarmed individual facing five gendarmes with submachine guns and semi-automatic pistols. Two of his men have lost control of themselves. The commander anticipates complications, the media outcry, the public reactions, the internal inquiries, the trial. Difficult to claim legitimate self-defense in such a case. The claim presupposes absolute necessity and proportionate response. In other words, that there was an attack on or threat to the life or bodily integrity of the officer or another person, that warnings were clearly given and that all means other than the use of weapons had proved impossible. One of the gendarmes, who has just taken the pulse of the man on the floor, announces that he is dead.

They remove his handcuffs and search him. They find a pocket knife in his sweatpants. The blade may be barely as long as the palm of a hand, but Travellers are known for the dexterity with which they handle them. They will say the individual attacked them. That he tried to stab one of them. It has to be in the neck, because it's the only part that is not protected by their body armor. They drag the body from the back of the lean-to toward the entrance, since he is supposed to have rushed toward them. They place the knife carefully, open, next to his extended hand. That the man attacked them with such a weapon is not enough, however, because they clearly had means other than firearms of subduing him. They need to show that they did everything possible to avoid getting to this point. The tasers. In the moment, the two gendarmes who carried them of course did not have time to use them because they were holding their semi-automatic pistols when the individual was discovered and their colleagues fired. But if they had used them, then they could have said that the individual had resisted the electric shocks and ripped the cables out. A reaction that is implausible, to be sure, but by no means totally impossible. Apparently, such exceptional cases have been known. They take off the blood-soaked tee-shirt. Two successive electric pulse gun charges shake the bare torso, three of the four darts embedding themselves. As for warnings before firing, if the events took place over such a short time and in such a confined space in the face of imminent danger, they will assert that it was impossible to give them. However, they will say that they asked the man to drop his weapon before he rushed them.

The story takes shape. The man stepped forward. The two gendarmes closest to him saw him holding a knife. Despite orders to drop it and taser shots to subdue him, he lunged at one of them, trying to stab him, forcing the second officer to fire to protect his comrade. The individual then turned toward the man who fired and dealt him a blow that threw him backward. Seeing them injured, and knowing that he in turn was in danger, the first officer

also had to fire to bring the crazed man under control,
who finally collapsed. The violence of the confrontation,
including the blow that knocked down the first shooter, is
backed up by evacuating him from the lean-to. Two gendarmes carry him outside, lay him down in the courtyard
and remove his bulletproof vest.

The members of the family have witnessed this scene
as if from the wings. The gendarmes entering the shed. A
few seconds of silence punctuated by the occasional sound
of someone bumping into an object. The burst of gunfire.
The barely audible moan. Then silence once more. Or
almost, as there is now whispering from inside the lumber
room. The consultation between the GIGN men goes on for
a while. It seems to them to last forever. They shout that
Angelo has been killed. They see gendarmes going in and
out, one of them holding a blood-soaked cloth, two others
carrying one of their colleagues. They try to find out, they
ask questions. No one answers them. But they guess. They
cry out their distress yet at the same time want to hold on
to hope. The father, uncle and brother are still face down
on the patio. The mother and sister-in-law are now sitting
on the steps of a caravan. The GIGN men tower over them,
terrifying in the assault gear that leaves only their eyes
visible. Witnessing the gendarmes' toing and froing, the
agitated activity in the shed, the muttered conversations,
the family understand that something is being stitched
together in the lean-to.

In the courtyard, the gendarmes have gathered together.
The first officer, convinced he fired the fatal shot, is still
in shock. The second officer has recovered more quickly
from his emotional reaction. The debriefing, broadened
to include the whole unit, serves to share the story of the
events and get it straight, so that those who were outside
can testify, depending on how far away they were, to what
they saw and, above all, heard – the noise of a fight and the
gendarmes' orders. It is important not to say that the decision to search the lean-to was made only after they heard
the noise of something falling because that would imply

that they might have guessed the target was in there and therefore that they should have adapted the intervention tactics, for example by negotiating with him to come out, or even by sending in a tear gas grenade, particularly given that the second officer had a gas mask, suggesting that this was a possible option once the objective had been discovered. Conversely, if the lumber room was investigated as part of a systematic search, the unexpectedness of the encounter and the inevitable outcome of the scene would be more easily believable.

This collective work of consolidating the story of the events does not prevent one or two unfortunate leaks, such as that from the emergency doctor who came to certify death, despite the fact that they had the foresight to make it clear to him how much his discretion would be appreciated. Nor does it avoid a few damaging discrepancies, as in the depositions during the immediate aftermath investigation, when the first officer who fired what was thought to be the fatal shot, clearly very shaken at the thought of the potential consequences of his action, repeated that he did not hear the man shout, whereas his colleague had described him roaring furiously, and that he had not seen the knife that the man was supposed to have been brandishing above him at the point when he fired. There are also regrettable improvisations, among others from the GIGN men who, hoping to make their account more realistic, quite imaginatively describe a boxing stance, a rugby scrum, or a struggle on the floor to grab the man's knife from him. More troublesome, a gap emerges between their statements on the evening of the events and the results of the autopsy conducted the next day. The gendarmes maintain that the man was standing in front of them, threatening them, and the two officers assert that they were facing him, at the same height, when they fired. The paths of the five bullets are clearly oriented from above to below, four of them entering the upper part of the thorax. The re-enactment in the presence of the protagonists, with ballistics experts in attendance, makes it possible partially to erase this inconsistency, however, since the new report states that the projectiles passed only slightly from above to below. This bending of the conclusions from the initial expert report should suffice to make the stories and the evidence concur on paper for purposes of the investigation.

Despite these complications, the version ultimately established seems to convince, or at least satisfy, the investigators and the public prosecutor. All have understood that what is at stake in the acceptance of legitimate self-defense is not only the likely dismissal of the case that the two who fired the fatal shots are hoping for, but also, as is the case each time such accidents occur, the protection of the moral authority of law enforcement – on two levels. First, admitting that Angelo did not defend himself with a weapon or attack the gendarmes, despite their warnings, but was killed without even having time to stand up would call into question the stories of the five who directly witnessed the events, and of others, including senior officers, who maintained that they heard the sounds of a fight, muffled shouts and orders. Second, acknowledging that the use of force was disproportionate, not to say unjustified given Angelo's criminal history, not only in the lean-to where eight bullets were fired at the chest of an unarmed man on his own but also in the decision to call in an assault unit in these circumstances, would jeopardize the work of the jewel in the national gendarmerie's crown. In short, if it was not shown that the man in the shed had attacked the officers, the misconduct of lying under oath would have been added to the violation of the rules of engagement. The account presented by the gendarmes, and accepted by the justice system, saves the honor of the institution.

So what did happen on the last day of Angelo's life, and how did this tragic dénouement come about? Justice made a decision. It produced its version of the facts. It called this version judicial truth. But, drawing on the same documents as the judges used, it proves possible to conceive of a different reading of the same facts. This reading has presupposed taking all the testimonies seriously, examining all the expert witness reports, not downplaying the inconsistencies, not concealing the contradictions. The aim has been to imagine what can be reasonably established from an analysis with no interest other than knowing and understanding. In this sense, it can of course be said that this account is simply an interpretation of the available verbal and written documents. But is the version formulated by the justice system not such an interpretation as well? With the major difference that this latter interpretation is considered true because it is sanctioned by a judicial ruling. Yet to take this version for truth is to forget that the account thus established still derives from a process of intellectual construction. It is also to forget that this construction is set within a field of power relations between institutions, and even within them. This is the other major difference from the version proposed here, which is not subject to these constraints.

The enormous advantage the official version has over all the other versions is its performative character. In articulating the law, it is supposed to articulate the truth. It seems self-evident to all as the only authorized version. But this legitimacy does not mean that it is the version that best holds up against the test of reality. Judicial truth does not necessarily deliver the account that rings most true. It does not exclude the possibility of seeking out a different interpretation of the facts. We might call it an ethnographic truth.

Epilogue

"Like a dog!" he said, it was as if the shame of it should outlive him.

Franz Kafka, *The Trial*

Angelo opens one eye. Looks at his watch. Seven o'clock. The sun has not yet risen, but through the windshield the first glimmers of daylight reveal a cloudless sky. A beautiful day in store. He unzips his sleeping bag. He notices that the air is not as cold as in the last few days. Spring is on its way. He wakes his son, who stretches. The car seats are not very comfortable, but they've gotten used to them over time. He pulls them back up and puts away his night gear. He pulls on his black sweatpants over the white ones, puts on his tee-shirt and sneakers. He looks at his son, who is also in the process of getting dressed. He examines himself in the rearview mirror, rubs his face, which shows straw marks from sleep, combs his hair with his fingers. He has nothing to eat. He has no money. As always, his pockets are empty. He's going to have to get someone to invite him for coffee. He takes his Subutex tablet, a heroin substitute medication, and slips it under his tongue. He waits a few minutes for it to dissolve completely. Then he puts on some music and turns the engine on. The vehicle pulls slowly out of the tree-lined track, turns onto the main road and moves toward his parents' house. He has not often visited them in the six months he has been out.

The car passes the last houses in the village and enters a narrow lane between uncultivated fields. He glimpses the welcoming silhouette of the family farm. He parks in a little rest area near the main building close to the road. Just as he gets out of the car, his sister opens the gate. She is just about to leave for her return-to-employment course, as she does every day. She tells him about the training in which she has enrolled, the basic skills she is learning, her hope of finding work at the hospital. He congratulates her on her plans. He says a few words to the children who are ready to go, one to elementary school, the others to day-care. He makes them laugh. He enters the courtyard. His parents are there, together with his young brother and his sister-in-law. They greet him affectionately, complain that he doesn't come to see them more frequently, invite him to stay to eat with them at the barbecue, as they are celebrating his brother's release from prison with an electronic tag. He accepts but says he has things to do and will come back around midday. Just as he is leaving, his father calls him back. He holds a black hat out to him. His hat. Angelo has often asked him for it. He beams. He places it proudly on his head and gets back on the road with his son. He goes to see his eldest daughter, who lives a few miles away. He tells her he is going to register at a job center to find work. He seems to have forgotten for a moment that he is sought as an absconder. He stays with her for a few minutes, then gets back to his car. A little further on, he stops on the side of the road, turns off the engine, rolls a joint, and smokes it as he chats with his son.

He restarts the engine and drives back toward his parents' home. He parks in front of the house. His son stays in the car, listening to music. He goes through the gate, sporting the paternal hat. He sees his mother, who tells him the men have gone to pick up identity documents and buy meat in a nearby town. He goes to fetch the charcoal and lights the fire. When his father, uncle and brother return shortly afterward, he is busy around the barbecue. He lets his brother and uncle take over and joins his father in the house. He asks him about his health, concerned at seeing him struggle for breath, his face suffused with purple, a green tube in his nose. Suddenly a loud noise – men in balaclavas rushing into the courtyard yelling orders. His father has stood up, he is in the doorway; he whispers to his son to go hide in the shed. Angelo slips behind him and disappears into the lean-to at the side of the house.

There, in the dark to which his eyes do not have time to adjust, he gropes his way between old planks, cast-off furniture, sundry second-hand appliances and boxes of comic books. Moving cautiously, he takes care to avoid the bicycle propped against the central beam and his father's oxygen bottle. He hides at the back of the space, behind a crate, under a plastic sheet. Throughout the noisy, methodical search of the house, he does not move a muscle. From his hideout, he hears everything. The uproar of the gendarmes in the family home, yelling at his parents to be quiet. His father's breathless moan, asking in vain for his medication as he is ordered to lie on the ground. His mother's stubborn refusal to answer the questions about where her son is. The door of his uncle's house kicked in on the other side of the courtyard. Well aware that he is the cause of this collective punishment inflicted on his family, Angelo trembles with rage. And also in fear of being found.

He holds his breath. Huddled in the darkness, he listens out. Now he has the impression that the operation is coming to an end. Outside, orders are no longer being shouted at his parents. The GIGN men seem to have moved off. He can only make out the muffled sound of their voices somewhere behind the caravan. They will be saying they haven't found him. His body is hurting. It's more than fifteen minutes that he has been crouching here without moving. Legs gone to sleep. He feels dizzy. He can't hold out any longer. He has to move a bit. Now he can. The danger seems to have passed. It looks as if the search has been halted. He stands up slowly, but his shoulder knocks an object, and the noise of its fall echoes in the lumber room. Angelo freezes, gripped by fright. The metallic sound went right through him. Did the gendarmes hear it? Maybe not. No one has rushed toward his hiding place. Outside everything is silent. But it is a strange silence. The gendarmes' conversation, which he heard in the distance, has stopped. Long seconds pass. Nothing happens.

Suddenly the door bursts open. Two figures appear in the opening. Angelo has crouched down again, doing his best to put his improvised hiding place against the wall back together again. He is blinded by the light from the doorway. He can just make out the eyes peering through the eyeholes in balaclavas under helmets, and he recognizes the heavy weapons held in firing position. He can see the two men, but they have not yet spotted him. Other figures emerge in the doorway. Moving forward into the room, the gendarmes stumble over obstacles. A beam of light sweeps the cluttered little space and comes to rest on the alcove where he is crouched. Angelo understands that he has been discovered. The two gendarmes are right in front of him. He wants to give himself up. He frees himself from the sheet that is partly covering him. Raises his hands and tries to stand. Does not have time to say anything. Does not even have time to stand up fully. A burst of gunfire, then another that hits him right in his chest. A final bullet hits his abdomen. He falls in the dust. Utters a brief moan.

He feels his hands being cuffed behind his back. As if that was still necessary. In the lean-to, gendarmes are coming in and out. They mill around, talking in low voices. Nobody thinks to give first aid. Beside him, an officer is talking, but he doesn't understand what he is saying. Blood is seeping from his wounds, flooding his tee-shirt, spreading over the floor. A sensation of cold sweeps over him. Yet, outside, the freshness of the morning is giving way to a gentle warmth. Perfect weather for a barbecue. The smell of grilled meat was already wafting on the air when the gendarmes arrived, interrupting this rare family reunion.

He thinks of his son. They have become inseparable over the course of these last few weeks on the run. Joined at the hip, as his mother likes to say. He wonders if the gendarmes arrested him before they came into the property a few minutes ago. Probably. They must have nabbed him by surprise when he was on his phone. Unless he saw them in time and was able to flee. Anyway, it's not his son they wanted. It's him. But why have they pulled out the big guns, sending in the GIGN? Why not just send gendarmes from the neighboring town, like they did for his brother? His thoughts are becoming clouded.

One day you'll see, they'll get you, his father had warned him a month earlier. The cops, they'll kill you. You'd be better off handing yourself in. But he couldn't go back to prison, it was too painful. After all these years, he was less and less able to stand being shut in. And there was that other sentence that would be activated. It would be long this time. And then, for sure, another on top for not returning from his home leave. Each time he appeared before the judge the sentence got longer. When the gendarmes had come to tell his parents that his brother had to go to the station to serve a sentence, his sister had suggested that he go along too and go back to finish his own. He had hesitated. If the prison administration granted him his relocation closer to his family, he and his brother might find themselves in the same jail. But his own sentence would be increased with a new one added. Maybe two. So he would be alone for several years. And he was well aware that he wouldn't get many visits. Not from his family, not from his friends, not from his ex-partners. So he decided against it. And anyway his father was in poor health. He wanted to be with him for the time he had left to live. He didn't want to be in prison when he died. He doubted, after what had happened, that he would be given home leave for the funeral. No, definitely, he would not hand himself in.

In the darkness of the shed, Angelo is dying. Alone. A few yards away from his father whom, despite himself, he has just subjected to this appalling ordeal and whose cries of despair he can now faintly make out. Around his body, from which life is seeping away, kitted and helmeted gendarmes are fussing about and whispering. Their movements and their voices are gradually fading away.

The old man was right, thinks Angelo. The cops, they got me.